100

THINGS TO DO IN
BLOOMINGTON
INDIANA
BEFORE YOU
DIE

Jenny,
See you
around
B-Town!

Heather Ray

Bloomington hiking and biking trail

100

THINGS TO DO IN
BLOOMINGTON
INDIANA
BEFORE YOU
DIE

• •

HEATHER RAY

REEDY PRESS

Copyright © 2023 by Reedy Press, LLC
Reedy Press
PO Box 5131
St. Louis, MO 63139, USA
www.reedypress.com

Library of Congress Control Number: 2023935436

ISBN: 9781681064543

Design by Jill Halpin

Photos by author unless otherwise noted.
Cover image courtesy of Abby Henkel at Beanblossom Bottoms Nature Preserve, a Sycamore Land Trust property.

Printed in the United States of America
23 24 25 26 27   5 4 3 2 1

DEDICATION

To George and Ellie, thank you for introducing me to the
Chocolate Moose.

Tibetan Mongolian Buddhist Cultural Center

CONTENTS

● ●

Music and Entertainment

● ●

Sports and Recreation

• •

Culture and History

● ●

Shopping and Fashion

• •

ACKNOWLEDGMENTS

To Ken, your adventurous spirit, kindness, goofiness, and love for the natural world are an inspiration. I love you. Thank you for your encouragement.

To the Cowley family, we appreciate you welcoming us to Bloomington and reminding me why I moved to Indiana the first two times.

To the townie friends and customers at our nature shop, Wild Birds Unlimited; this book would not exist without your tips, advice, and deep-rooted knowledge of and love for Bloomington.

To our above-and-beyond staff, Sasha and Mallory, thanks for the many suggestions and ideas, and for being the "persons in charge" during crunch time and all the time.

To Amanda Doyle, I'm so glad we reconnected for more writing adventures about Indiana. I'm grateful for knowing you and for the support from Reedy Press.

To my family and friends across the country, thank you for your encouragement from afar. Now you have 100 more reasons to come visit. See you soon.

PREFACE

Admittedly, I've moved to Indiana twice before, and both experiences were without question some of the best years of my life. But it's true what they say, third time's the charm. When my husband and I settled in Bloomington, it felt like home from day one, thanks in large part to close townie friends. Nothing says welcome to Bloomington like unloading the U-Haul and heading straight to Mother Bear's Pizza to celebrate a 7th birthday. The very next weekend we found ourselves outside Memorial Stadium tailgating with the best of them, and I'm grateful to say, the adventures have been nonstop ever since.

As a writer and editor for more than 20 years, I've had the pleasure of sharing places to go, things to do, and what to eat for magazines, cookbooks, and digital publications, mostly centered on the Midwest. And now with a sole focus on Bloomington, I have the honor of doing that to celebrate a place my husband and I call "our forever home."

But make no mistake, this book was not curated by my newcomer eyes alone. It's a reflection of insider townie advice with a shared passion for wanderlust. This book is for newcomers and visitors looking to explore Bloomington as well as longtime residents hosting out-of-towners and in the mood for a little inspiration.

It's the people, local businesses, Hoosier culture, and nature—along with those who protect it—that make this place so endearing. Did I mention the food? Did I mention the arts, entertainment, sports, history, and shopping? Let's get started.

• •

FOOD
AND DRINK

GET A TASTE OF HISTORY 101
AT BUFFALOUIE'S

Both history buffs and wing aficionados will find something to love at this iconic B-Town wing and burger spot. In 1927, Hoagy Carmichael composed the revered song "Stardust" in this very building when it housed a different but no less popular student hangout called the Book Nook. Fast forward 100 years and the campus energy carries on behind the structure's gabled facade, especially on game days. This is the place to soak in Hoosier memorabilia while sharing a platter of wings and fries and cheering on the home team. And if you're questioning the authenticity of wings in the Hoosier state, you can take comfort in knowing the founder was an IU student native to Buffalo, New York.

114 S Indiana Ave., 812-333-3030
buffalouies.com

TIP
Look for the statue of Hoagy Carmichael near the northeast corner of the IU Auditorium on East 7th Street. The sculpture of this Bloomington native and legendary songwriter toured Indiana before settling in on campus. The sculpture was created by IU graduate Michael McAuley.

HEAD DOWNTOWN
TO UPTOWN CAFE

Ask any Bloomington foodie to name the top restaurants in Bloomington, and Uptown will be on the list. Opened by Chef Michael Cassady in 1976, this former breakfast diner has evolved into a dining destination serving upscale Creole-inspired fare in the heart of Bloomington. Residents and visitors alike race to get a table for brunch while others prefer the lower-key breakfasts served on weekdays. For dinner this is a great spot for steak or cajun. Think shrimp and grits, gumbo, and red beans and rice. For dinner, reservations are recommended as this is a popular place for graduation dinners, anniversaries, and birthdays, in addition to being a favored spot for foodies. However, they don't accept reservations for Saturday or Sunday brunch—so go early.

102 E Kirkwood Ave., 812-339-0900
the-uptown.com

TIP

Steak lovers (and spicy meatball lovers) will also appreciate Janko's Little Zagreb at 223 West 6th Street. It's known for its high-end menu and charming red and white decor. Or for a white-tablecloth celebration, make a reservation at Truffles for a modern fine dining experience.

B-LINE IT
TO CARDINAL SPIRITS DISTILLERY

Bloomington's first artisan distillery is one of many favorite attractions along the B-Line trail, and not just because of the award-winning booze. Well, mostly because of the award-winning booze. The food, service, and occasional board game night or live show are also worth the trip. It's true that Cardinal Spirits liquors can be found in stores around the country, but isn't it better to go straight to the source, where experts can mix up a seasonal or signature cocktail for you? Everything is made from scratch using local ingredients whenever possible, including the lunch and dinner menus. And if you love brunch, especially a boozy brunch (no judgment here), mark your calendar for Sundays and indulge in an eclectic menu. Or if you're more of the lazy Sunday morning type, be sure to pick up a pack of canned cocktails to enjoy at your leisure.

922 S Morton St., 812-202-6789
cardinalspirits.com

SINK THE BIZ
AT NICK'S ENGLISH HUT

When people say "the heart of Bloomington," they mean Nick's, serving up a good time since 1926. Today, this quintessential bar is an institution for students, residents, returning alumni, and more than a few celebrities. It's where fans high-five on game days and couples celebrate wedding receptions. And then there's a little game folks like to play called Sink the Biz. Here's how it works: A highball glass is placed in a bucket of beer. Players take turns pouring beer in the glass, and if you sink the glass, you drink the contents. Got it? Now go. While you're there, be sure to check out the wall of fame, which includes a signature from President Obama. Over the years, other celebs like Mark Cuban, Kurt Vonnegut, and John Mellencamp have also walked through the doors.

423 E Kirkwood Ave., 812-332-4040
nicksenglishhut.com

TIP
Under the same ownership as Nick's is Osteria Rago, a hidden gem for Italian food. Find it tucked inside an 1880s-style carriage house in the alley between Kirkwood Avenue and 6th Street. Discover grand-mother-style cooking featuring house-made pasta, deli sandwiches, and wood-fired pizzas.

ASK FOR CANDY EYES
AT THE CHOCOLATE MOOSE

Nothing brings a smile to a child's face faster than when there's ice cream staring back at them. This works for adults, too. Especially at the Chocolate Moose, where you can get candy googly eyes on your favorite flavors. (Hint: it's usually the Grasshopper.) By now, most townies either have fond memories of taking their kids here or being taken as kids themselves. The Chocolate Moose as we know it has been operating since 1983, but its origins date back to the 1930s, when it operated as May's Cafe. It was pared down to an ice cream parlor to survive the depression and has since changed names and ownership, but today it's evolved into a traditional way to treat yourself, the family, or visitors to a sweet little scoop of Bloomington.

405 S Walnut St., 812-333-0475
moosebtown.com

TIP
The Chocolate Moose serves a full menu of hot sandwiches for breakfast, lunch, and dinner, including a local favorite—hot dogs with homemade coney sauce.

SWEET SCOOPS

Brilliant Coffee Company
A selection of brightly colored
and brilliantly flavored gelatos.
217 W 6th St., 812-668-2925
brilliantcoffeeco.com

Brusters
A popular walk-up ice cream stand serving
scoops made on-site. (Open seasonally)
4531 E 3rd St., 812-331-8979
brusters.com

Hartzell's Ice Cream
Handcrafted ice cream made in small batches.
107 N Dunn St., 812-332-3502
hartzellsicecream.com

Jiffy Treet East
A Bloomington tradition with
indoor and outdoor seating.
223 S Pete Ellis Dr., Ste. 3A, 812-339-9981
facebook.com/jiffytreeteast

Jiffy Treet West
An Ellettsville gathering place with
a drive-thru and outdoor seating.
4727 W State Rd. 46, 812-876-7770
jiffytreet.com

TASTE A VEGAN DONUT
AT RAINBOW BAKERY

You don't have to be vegan to appreciate a freshly baked treat, but if you are, this place is the literal jackpot at the end of the rainbow. Since 2013, this all-vegan bakery has been serving residents and students an assortment of goodies that come in thoughtful flavors, like blueberry lemon, sweet coconut curry, the Homer (strawberry with sprinkles), and dozens more. And that's just the donuts, many of which are also gluten-free. The walk-up case inside this retro-inspired space also features a selection of colorful cupcakes, cookies, brownies, muffins, and oatmeal cream pies. If those don't make your eyes pop, check out the staff's art displayed on the wall. While you're there, grab a pound of coffee beans to go. The beans are roasted just a hop, skip, and jump away at Hopscotch Coffee Roastery.

201 S Rogers St., 812-822-3741
rainbowbakery.net

TIP
You can never have enough freshly baked treats. Two Sticks Bakery on North Washington Street is also worth a trip. This women-owned bakery bakes fresh goodies throughout the morning, but the best advice is to go early and stock up.

SIP HARD CIDER
AT FRIENDLY BEASTS

Try hard cider like you've never tasted before when you belly up to the bar or grab a table at Friendly Beasts Cider Company. This is not the kind of sweet, store-bought cider you may be familiar with. The ciders here are fermented locally using Indiana apples and traditional cider-making methods. Expect most of the ciders to be on the drier side, but with such a large variety of styles to choose from you're bound to find something to please every taste bud in the group. Creative blends of ginger, fruit, or honey produce flavors like the Ginger Snapper, Screech Owl Peach, or Buzzed Boomer. Order a flight of five varieties to sample; once you find your favorite, fill a growler to take home.

222 W 2nd St., 812-641-5553
friendlybeastscider.com

TIP
The public taproom is located in the Made building of Artisan Alley along the B-Line trail. The entrance is on the west side, facing the trail.

ORDER PORK TENDERLOIN
AT THE CABIN RESTAURANT & LOUNGE

On your way to or from Lake Monroe, stop by the Cabin Restaurant & Lounge along State Highway 446. This unassuming roadside diner and bar is home to an iconic oversized breaded pork tenderloin, an Indiana favorite. Here they do it right. It's the kind of sandwich that hangs way too far outside of the bun in an almost comical way. Another popular menu option is to order the pork tenderloin tucked under a serving of smothered biscuits and gravy. The Cabin also has a full bar and pool tables and does open mic nights, hosts karaoke, and has live music on select evenings. On warm-weather nights, the patio is a great spot to unwind with a group of friends. First-timers can expect a warm welcome from staff and friendly regulars.

4015 S St. Rd. 446, 812-323-9654
cabinrestaurant446.com

CELEBRATE A BIRTHDAY
AT MOTHER BEAR'S PIZZA

Your style of pizza preference is personal, and Mother Bear's Pizza understands. Deep-dish, traditional pan, thin crust—you can get it all here. This popular pizza haunt started pumping out pies near campus back in 1973 to serve the owners' original business down the street, Bear's Place. Yes, they would walk hot pizza down the street. But once word spread and awards started rolling in, Mother Bear's achieved celebrity status and eventually opened a second location on the west side with a similar vibe, complete with guests' graffitied signatures on the walls. Today this family-friendly pizzeria is a hotspot for celebrating birthdays, as the tradition of getting a discount based on your age continues. Know anyone turning 100 this year?

Campus: 1428 E 3rd St., 812-332-4495
West: 2980 W Whitehall Crossing Blvd., 812-287-7366
motherbearspizza.com

DINE
IN THE ENTIRE TOWN
OF STORY, INDIANA

Make a reservation for a prix fixe dinner or stay for brunch after an overnight stay at the Story Inn. It's true that the entire town of Story is located within this former general store turned boutique hotel with just over a dozen renovated rooms and cottages. Founded in 1851, the village of Story was once a bustling settlement with a church, two general stores, a school, a grain mill, a sawmill, a slaughterhouse, a blacksmithing forge, and a post office. However, the town struggled to recover after the Great Depression, and much of the land was sold to form nearby Brown County State Park. Today, Story is listed on the National Register of Historic Places and has become a destination for curious visitors and foodies. They also host live entertainment throughout the year.

6404 Indiana Hwy. 135, Nashville, 812-988-2273
storyinn.com

TIP
Do you believe in ghosts? Be on the lookout for the "Blue Lady." Old Story Inn guest books are riddled with accounts of paranormal activity. The ghost is described as wearing a long white gown and having piercing blue eyes, and she reportedly leaves blue items in her wake.

CHOOSE FUNKY TOPPINGS
AT THE ORBIT ROOM

You could do several laps around the Courthouse Square without ever noticing the narrow stairwell next to JL Waters gear shop. But if you're hungry for the most eclectic hotdogs in town, find your way down the stairs and belly up to the bar at the Orbit Room. Regulars come here for trivia, gamers come for pinball, songwriters come for the music, artists come for the vibe, and everyone comes for the menu. House-made hotdog toppings like garlic whipped cheese, spiced peanuts, and vegan miso aioli are among more than a dozen ways to top your frank, which can be ordered vegan or vegetarian. Be sure to check their events page. This niche basement bar fills up fast.

107 N College Ave., Ste. 001, 812-369-4130
orbitbtown.com

TIP
Only in the mood for food? Place an order online for pickup. The Orbit Room is all ages until 8 p.m.

EAT CRÊPES FROM THE WINDOW
AT LE PETIT CAFÉ

Experience authentic Provincial cuisine when you walk up to the window on Saturday mornings at Le Petit Café. This is where owners Patrick and Marina literally open up their kitchen window to serve passersby on the B-Line trail. One mustn't be afraid of butter or cream. This is French fare at its finest, and you never know what might be on special for the day. Although crêpes, croissants, and some delicious egg dishes often make the menu, occasionally the chefs get creative with a bottle of booze. Bourbon bread pudding anyone? While the dining room is no longer serving dinner after 45 years of heartfelt service, Bloomingtonians are encouraged to stop by the Saturday morning window and say *bonjour*!

308 W 6th St., 812-334-9747
facebook.com/lepetitcafebloomington

TIP
From the cafe window, follow the B-Line trail north just two blocks and catch live music at the Saturday morning farmers market.

POUR YOUR OWN BEAR OF HONEY
AT HUNTER'S BEE FARM

Take the trip about 30 miles north of downtown Bloomington for a tour of Hunter's Bee Farm, which has been producing honey since 1910. Owners Tracy and Chris Hunter are fourth-generation beekeepers, and along with their team of worker bees, they manage 65 acres of hardwood timber, including thousands upon thousands of bees. Choose from a variety of tours that may include beeswax candle rolling, honey tasting, beekeeper demonstrations, and bottling your own honey bear—a generous six-ounce pour with your own personal label. In addition to producing honey, the farm also uses beeswax and pollen to make an assortment of tempting products in the gift shop. Make a reservation online or by phone and get ready for a sweet treat.

6501 W Honey Ln., Martinsville, 765-537-9430
huntershoneyfarm.com

TIP
The property is also home to a variety of pines. During the holiday months, visitors can cut their own Christmas tree or choose from a selection of pre-cut trees.

EAT YOUR VEGGIES
AT THE OWLERY

Owls may not be vegetarian, but everything on the menu at this Hogwarts-inspired eatery is plant-based. Two musicians with a fondness for Harry Potter books, Toby Foster and Ryan Woods, opened the restaurant in 2011 to meet the demand of the growing vegetarian and vegan community in Bloomington. Here you can order vegetarian counterparts to classic comfort foods like poutine, loaded nachos, or a hot reuben sandwich, and everything on the menu can be made vegan. Wash it down with a local beer on tap or warm up with hot tea. On nice-weather days, bring the dog and snag an outdoor table with views of the Courthouse Square. Oh, and you don't have to be vegetarian; you just have to like really delicious food.

118 W 6th St., 812-333-7344
theowleryrestaurant.com

TIP
A special brunch menu is served on Sundays. Say yum to pancakes, waffles, biscuits and gravy, breakfast sandwiches, and more.

SAVOR HIMALAYAN FOOD
ON "INTERNATIONAL ROW"

Take a stroll down 4th Street heading west from South Dunn Street. This is "International Row," where you can pick just about any restaurant and dig into something authentic to its origins. Within just a few short blocks you'll find Burmese, Cajun, Greek, Indian, Korean, Thai, and Bloomington's only Tibetan restaurant, Anyetsang's Little Tibet. Here you'd be remiss not to order the pillowy Tibetan dumplings called momo. Owner Pema Wangchen, a Tibetan refugee and former monk with a storied past full of long journeys on foot, took over the restaurant from his uncle in 2013. In addition to a menu of home-cooked Himalayan food, diners can expect a homelike dining room trimmed with Tibetan decor.

415 E 4th St., 812-331-0122
anyetsangs.com

TIP
In addition to Tibentian food, Little Tibet also serves Thai and Indian specialties.

COZY UP
IN A LOCAL COFFEE SHOP

One of the many perks of being in a college town is that there's no shortage of coffee. If you're in the mood for something luxurious, swing by Brilliant Coffee Co. and add a cup of homemade gelato to your order. For a morning meal, hang out on the porch overlooking the B-Line trail at Hopscotch Coffee on Dodds Street. At Soma Coffeehouse and Juice Bar, it's a tough decision between a frothy drink, a whole-fruit smoothie, or organic juice. On the East side of town, try Needmore (named after the owner's elementary school in Springville, Indiana), where beans are ethically sourced and roasted in small batches. At Crumble or Verona, a baked good is a must, and at the Inkwell Bakery and Cafe, you'll eat and drink very well, especially if you order their take on a popular rectangular childhood pastry.

TIP

Poindexter, the lobby-level coffee bar at the Graduate Hotel downtown, is a popular spot to curl up with a book or order a nostalgic treat like milk and cookies.

PERK UP AT A COFFEE SHOP

Brilliant Coffee Company
217 W 6th St., 812-668-2925
brilliantcoffeeco.com

Crumble Coffee & Bakery
1567 S Piazza Dr., 812-334-9044
532 N College Ave., 812-287-8056
316 S Swain Ave., 812-822-1679
crumblecoffee.square.site

Hopscotch Coffee
235 W Dodds St., Ste. 2, 812-369-4500
212 N Madison St., 812-287-7767
hopscotchcoffee.com

The Inkwell
105 N College Ave., 812-822-2925
401 S Woodlawn Ave., 812-287-8354
inkwellbtown.com

Needmore Coffee Roasters
104 N Pete Ellis Dr., Ste. E, 812-727-0204
needmoreroasters.com

Poindexter
210 E Kirkwood Ave., 812-994-0500
graduatehotels.com/bloomington/restaurant/poindexter

Soma Coffeehouse & Juice Bar
1400 E 3rd St., 812-333-7334
322 E Kirkwood Ave., 812-331-2770
581 E Hillside Dr., Ste. 104, 812-668-2086
iheartsoma.com

Verona Coffee House
3105 S Sare Rd., Ste. 101, 812-676-6358
veronacoffeehouse.com

BE CHARMED
BY THE TCHOTCHKES
AT THE RUNCIBLE SPOON

Everyone has that one funky friend in Bloomington whose house is layered with tchotchkes, plants, and tightly packed bookcases. A meal at the Runcible Spoon is like dining at that friend's house, as long as that person makes pancakes the size of your head and serves breakfast all day. This townie hotspot has been serving up tasty bites since 1976 and is adored for its eclectic yet still cozy atmosphere, freshly roasted coffee, and expanded menu that now serves lunch and dinner in addition to their famous breakfast and brunch. With patios in the front and back, basement seating, and an upstairs, there are plenty of options for finding a favorite table. As for the trinket-rich decor, it's based on the story of the Runcible Spoon.

412 E 6th St., 812-334-3997
runciblespoonrestaurant.com

TIP

Did someone say breakfast all day? B-Town Diner, the Village Deli, Cozy Table, and Cloverleaf are among the go-tos for diner-style pancakes, biscuits and gravy, eggs, and more. All. Day. Long. Or at least for as long as they're open in a day.

HAVE A BURGER AND SHAKE
AT HINKLE'S HAMBURGERS

This famous Bloomington burger joint has been flipping patties since 1930 and has been voted the best burger in town, no easy feat considering the number of tasty burgers around. What makes it so good? It's the perfect storm of small town charm, friendly service, and fresh ground beef mixed with onions sizzling on the grill. Add a milkshake and a side of tater cakes or onion rings and discover your new happy place. After being family-owned and managed for more than 85 years, the restaurant closed in 2019. But thanks to new owners, local couple Richie and Janna Shields, the iconic hotspot reopened with a mission to serve the same great burgers and shakes they too have loved for years.

206 S Adams St., 812-339-3335
facebook.com/hinkleshamburgers

TIP

Hungry for a challenge? Try the Big Ugly at Bub's Burgers and Ice Cream on North Morton Street downtown. Diners who finish this enormous one-pound burger (weight is after it's cooked) get their picture on the wall. Good luck saving room for ice cream.

IMBIBE ON THE PATIO
AT UPLAND'S ORIGINAL BREWPUB

Bring the dog, bring the kids, and always bring out-of-town guests to experience the patio at Upland's original brewpub. Upland Brewing Company is among the largest brewers in Indiana and perhaps most famous for the best-selling Dragonfly IPA. Spring through fall, pull up a chair under an umbrella on a sunny afternoon or dine under the strung patio lights in the evening and enjoy a full lunch and dinner menu inspired by local ingredients. Beer lovers, if you're looking for something new and puckery for your palate, book a tour at the Wood Shop next door, where Upland brewers produce barrel-aged sours in a world-class facility. As the story goes, in 2006 Upland traded beer for barrels from Oliver Winery and has been successfully experimenting with sour beers ever since.

350 W 11th St., 812-364-2337
uplandbeer.com

BLOOMINGTON BREWERIES

Bloomington Brewing Company
Bloomington's first craft brewery; their beer is available
at Lennie's and area bars and restaurants.
2234 W Industrial Park Dr., 812-822-1760
bloomingtonbrew.com

Metal Works Brewing Company
A rotating selection of small-batch
beer and a full food menu.
108 E 6th St., 812-676-1000
metalworksbrewingcompany.com

Switchyard Brewing Company
Family-friendly gathering place with
food available from Estación D Sabor.
419 N Walnut St., 812-287-8295
switchyardbrewing.com

The Tap
More than a dozen original beers
brewed on site and traditional pub fare.
101 N College Ave., 812-287-8579
thetapbeerbar.com

PICNIC IN STYLE
AT A LOCAL WINERY

Two of the most picturesque places to have a picnic in
Bloomington just happen to be at local wineries. Oliver
Winery, off I-69 about eight miles north of downtown, is the
largest winery in Indiana and among the top 50 in the country.
Beautifully manicured gardens and water features surround
the tasting room and create a magical backdrop for sampling
wine and a basket of goodies. Guests can bring their own picnic
or call to reserve a picnic package. At Butler Winery, nine
miles northeast of downtown, visitors can grab a patio table
overlooking the vineyards while tasting estate-grown wine.
Order off the charcuterie menu or bring your own picnic to
enjoy at your table or down by the pond. If you time it right,
you might even catch live music in the pavilion. Cheers.

Oliver Winery
200 E Winery Rd., 812-876-5800
oliverwinery.com

Butler Winery
6200 E Robinson Rd., 812-332-6660
butlerwinery.com

TIP
Make your own! The downtown Butler Winery tasting room on North
College carries a selection of beer and winemaking supplies. Or you
can simply enjoy a drink in the wine garden.

"SPEAK EASY"
AT THE DUNNKIRK LIBRARY

Looking for a quiet place to sip a craft cocktail? Head to the Dunnkirk Library, if you can find it, and speak quietly with a friend. The Dunnkirk Library is Bloomington's hidden speakeasy-esque bar, tucked away in the back of the Upstairs Pub on Kirkwood. Once inside this stylish, low-key space, choose from a variety of themed menu collections, like the Literary Libations menu, where you can order the Hemingway Special, or get a Sidecar from the True Classics menu. For special effects, order a How About Them Apples and watch the bartender's performance go up in smoke. For Guinness drinkers, scan the QR code on the menu and choose what design you want in your beer foam. Before you know it, you'll be in Instagram heaven, toasting friends with a frothy or a still-smokin' cocktail in hand.

430 E Kirkwood Ave., Ste. 18, 812-606-2449
dunnkirklibrary.com

TIP
Reservations are recommended and gussied up attire is encouraged.

DINE
HARRY POTTER–STYLE
AT THE TUDOR ROOM

Located down an unassuming hallway inside the Indiana Memorial Union, you'll find the prestigious Tudor Room. Walking inside, fans of Harry Potter will feel all the wizardry vibes radiating from the opulent dining hall. Many diners describe it as a real-life Hogwarts. Dripping with collegiate elegance, from the heraldic banners representing IU's campus departments to the dramatic floor-to-ceiling stained glass windows and the luxuriant chandeliers, the space was designed to mimic a grand 15th-century English dining experience. And the buffet is equally majestic, serving weekday lunches and Sunday brunches that are considered tradition for many families. Friendly service, table linens, lavish desserts—it's all part of the Tudor Room experience. Parking is available in the Indiana Memorial Union pay lots. Customers can ask their server for a discounted voucher.

900 E 7th St., 812-855-1620
imu.indiana.edu/restaurants/tudor-room/index.html

TIP

Looking for an outdoor brunch option? Head to Scenic View. From your patio table, enjoy sweeping views of Hoosier National Forest with a shimmering glimpse of Lake Monroe while you toast with a signature Bloody Mary.

SIT ON THE FLOOR
AT TURKUAZ CAFE

Expect to be greeted and welcomed like family, and prepare yourself for a warming meal. The first thing you'll notice is the cozy living area to your right. Here you can kick off your shoes and cozy up on the low pillowy couches for a first date or an evening with friends. If dining close to the floor isn't your thing, grab a table with actual chairs in the back. Either way, you're in for an authentically Turkish meal, starting with spiced lentil soup and ending with Turkish coffee and baklava freshly drizzled with honey. In between, choose from a variety of Turkish pide; it's a soft bread stuffed with meats, veggies, or both. Like pizza shops in the US, pide restaurants can be found throughout Turkey, and lucky for us, we have one in Bloomington.

301 E 3rd St., 812-333-7908

TIP
Find a home-cooked Turkish brunch buffet, complete with authentic sweet and savory options, at Sofra Cafe on S Walnut St.

EAT FRIED CATFISH
AT THE PORTHOLE INN

Lake Lemon's neighborhood bar and grill in Unionville is not just a local hangout—it's a boater's paradise. Whether you park a pontoon out back at the new dock (which can fit about three boats on each side), or pull into a parking spot in the gravel lot out front, dropping in for a cold beer and platter of fried catfish is equivalent to après-ski for lake goers. The family-friendly gathering place for neighbors, families, and lake visitors has been around for more than 60 years and was recently bought by a group of friends who want to keep the many traditions of the Porthole Inn alive. One of those is the restaurant's famous pizza oven. Another is live music, and a third is the inevitable dancing that happens after a pitcher has been ordered.

8939 E S Shore Dr., Unionville, 812-339-1856

TIP

Lake Lemon is also home to The Little Africa Wildlife Viewing Area, a short trail and viewing platform that offers glimpses of the 25-acre peninsula on the far eastern end of the lake. For birders, this is a shorebird hotspot during spring and fall migration.

The Bluebird
Photo courtesy of Visit Bloomington

MUSIC
AND ENTERTAINMENT

SEE STARS
IN THE MAKING
WITH CONSTELLATION
STAGE AND SCREEN

In 2022, stars aligned when three theater and film organizations joined forces to become Constellation Stage and Screen. One of them, the Bloomington Playwrights Project, was the first theater company in the state to produce only original plays. Now combined with classic musicals and film, each Constellation season promises to feature original works, holiday favorites, and a new generation of exciting films. Performances and screenings take place at several local venues, including the historic Waldron building in the Courthouse Square Historic District. The 1915 building once served as Bloomington's city hall and later the headquarters of the police and fire departments. Since being deeded to Bloomington Area Arts Council, the space has been transformed into a performing arts space and gallery.

Box office: 812-336-9300
seeconstellation.org

TIP

Are you ready to be a star? Sign up for a Constellation improv class. Film production and acting classes are also available.

APPLAUD
A PERFORMANCE
AT THE BUSKIRK-CHUMLEY THEATER

In 1922, the Buskirk-Chumley, then called "the Indiana," opened its doors for its very first movie screening. Nearly 1,300 Bloomington residents showed up for the theater's debut of *The Storm*, a silent film starring Virginia Valli. Now, more than 100 years later, the landmark theater on Kirkwood has seen a few things. It survived fire damage, changes in ownership, and fierce local competition, and it was even closed for several years before it was donated to the Bloomington Area Arts Council, at which point it received generous donations and volunteer support. Today, it's a true community performing arts space that proudly serves as the main stage for a number of festivals and welcomes both local and national touring acts to the stage. From world-renowned musicians to local plays and animated films, there's no shortage of entertainment within this historical place.

114 E Kirkwood Ave., 812-323-3020
buskirkchumley.org

MEET UP
AT FOOD TRUCK FRIDAY

Warm summer days are meant for dining al fresco and enjoying ice cream. Enter Food Truck Friday at Switchyard Park. Once a week between April and October, a rotating selection of vendors line the pavilion to serve tasty food while crowds listen to live music and take advantage of the many park amenities. Send the kids to the playground, take the pup to the dog park, or hop on the B-Line trail for a walk, jog, or bike ride. Parking at the pavilion is a breeze, and while there are plenty of public tables, it's not a bad idea to bring your own lawn chair. If you time it right, you might catch another show in the nearby amphitheater. Word to the wise: if you're the type that wants to eat right away (me), go early to beat the lines before things get rockin' and rollin'. Follow @FoodTruckFriday on Facebook for an updated list of vendors.

1601 S Rogers St., 317-439-3903
facebook.com/foodtruckfriday

WATCH THE BIG SCREEN UNDER THE STARS
AT THE STARLITE DRIVE-IN

Pack the lawn chairs and frisbees and head to the Starlite Drive-In. As one of only around 300 operating drive-in theaters left in the United States, this retro Bloomington experience is one to appreciate. Some prefer to go early and grab dinner at the newly expanded concession stand or throw frisbees and footballs in the lot before the show. You can sit outside in camp chairs, cozy up in a hatchback, or enjoy the show from the driver's seat with the radio tuned to 97.5 FM. For most weekend showings, the admission price includes a double feature. Tickets can be purchased on site or online. The season typically runs early spring through mid fall.

7640 S Old Indiana 37, 812-824-2277
starlitebloomington.com

TIP

For more outdoor movie fun, check out the City of Bloomington Parks and Recreation Movies in the Parks series. Find the schedule at bloomington.in.gov/parks/events/concerts.

SEE A SHOW
AT THE INDIANA UNIVERSITY AUDITORIUM

In the late 1930s, while other universities around the country were cutting funding for the arts, IU president Herman B. Wells was busy building what would become an esteemed institute for performing arts, including one of the world's top music schools and the acclaimed Indiana University Auditorium—a 3,200-seat theater that today hosts a diverse roster of performances. A season's schedule likely includes comedians, magicians, lecturers, and musicians. The venue has hosted His Holiness the 14th Dalai Lama of Tibet, the Metropolitan Opera, Jerry Seinfeld, Bob Dylan, and Broadway musicals like *My Fair Lady* and *The Book of Mormon*. Tickets for all shows can be purchased online, in person at the IU Auditorium box office, and by phone.

1211 E 7th St., 812-855-1103
iuauditorium.com

TIP

Plan to spend a few extra minutes wandering the Hall of Murals, where artist Thomas Hart Benton detailed Indiana's cultural history in a series of captivating large-scale panels.

BE WOWED
AT THE MAC

If you're new to Bloomington, you may not know that some of the most talented student opera and ballet performers in the world study at Indiana University's renowned Jacobs School of Music. Proof of this can be seen in one of the grandest performance venues in the United States, the Musical Arts Center (MAC) on campus. Inside the theater, the first thing you'll notice is the main stage, stretching 90 feet wide and 60 feet deep—the ideal backdrop for dramatic scenic designs. It's perhaps one of many reasons why the school attracts creative and musical directors from around the globe. Because of the sizeable stage, of the 1,460 seats, there's not a bad one in the house.

101 N Eagleson Ave., 812-855-7433
operaballet.indiana.edu

TIP
Get to know local opera star Sylvia McNair when you browse nearly 5,000 items of collected work in the Sylvia McNair Digital Collection. The two-time Grammy Award-winning singer received a Master of Music with Distinction from the Jacobs School of Music, where she later returned to teach. Check it out at collections.libraries.indiana.edu/iulibraries.

CATCH
A HARD-TO-FIND FLICK
AT INDIANA UNIVERSITY CINEMA

Academy Award–winning actress Meryl Streep was once quoted saying, "The IU Cinema is one of the finest projection houses I have ever seen: state-of-the-art sight and sound facilities enclosed in a beautiful building." This stunning movie palace was built in 1930 and was originally used to host university theater productions. Now, with its 260 seats, massive screen, 14 surround-sound speakers, and murals on either side of the theater, it's an ideal venue to seek inspiration from movies ranging from silent classics to the latest pop culture hits. And because it also has an orchestra pit, you can occasionally catch a silent film with live musical accompaniment from orchestras and musicians from the Jacobs School of Music. Screenings are open to the public. Some, but not all, are free.

1213 E 7th St., 812-856-2463
cinema.indiana.edu

STAY UP LATE
AT THE BLUEBIRD

What do John Mellencamp, Lou Reed, and John Prine have in common, besides being music legends? They all once surprised a crowd of around 100 concert-goers in 1987 at the Bluebird nightclub, Bloomington's storied rock venue. It was a historical moment that townies still talk about (and one that has since been released on YouTube). During any given performance at the Bluebird, you're guaranteed all the rock-on vibes this place is now known for. Interestingly, the Bluebird opened as a non-music bar in 1973 before becoming a jazz club and eventually evolving into an all-genre music venue. Shows range from up-and-coming musicians to crowd-favorite tribute bands. But don't expect anyone to take the stage before 9 or 10 p.m.

216 N Walnut St., 812-336-3984
thebluebird.ws

TIP
Before the show, grab a bite to eat and take in the cream and crimson pride at nearby Yogi's Bar & Grill.

TREASURE HUNT
FOR NEW AND USED
VINYL, CDS, AND CASSETTES

From Kirkwood to South Walnut, you never know what you'll find at several new and used record shops, all within walking distance to one another. One of them, TD's CDs & LPs, may require a literal treasure map, as this hidden basement shop is tucked underneath Parlor Doughnuts (yum, by the way) and is accessible via the iron gate off Kirkwood, or through the back room of Soma Coffee Shop. Once inside, you'll strike it rich with hard-to-find albums from around the globe. Heading east on Kirkwood, you'll find Tracks, an eclectic shop with a variety of records hiding beyond a sea of cream and crimson IU gear. Heading back west, make a left on Walnut and discover Landlocked Music, where you'll find rows of new and used records with the option to special order any treasures you don't find in store.

TD's CDs & LPs
322 E Kirkwood Ave., Ste. 21, 812-322-9920

Tracks
415 E Kirkwood Ave., 812-332-3576

Landlocked Music
115 S Walnut St., 812-339-2574
landlockedmusic.com

SING KARAOKE
AT THE OFFICE LOUNGE
AND LIQUOR STORE

This darling dive bar is not your father's office break room. In fact, if it's after 10 p.m. on Friday or Saturday, it's time to take the stage and sing your heart out at the famous bar-meets-liquor-store. The Office Lounge is a neighborhood favorite for after-work drinks and serious comfort food. Think fried pickles, breaded tenderloin sandwiches, and steak that won't break the bank. It's a hotspot for nearby residents, yet everyone is welcome with open arms and cold brews. Order a pitcher of beer, shoot some pool, and escape the college bar scene at this hometown watering hole. And a couple nights a week, you can try your hand at Texas hold 'em. Can't stay? Pop in for takeout and a six-pack from the adjoining carryout liquor store.

3900 E 3rd St., 812-332-0911
officeloungeandliquorstore.com

LAUGH THE NIGHT AWAY
AT THE COMEDY ATTIC

The only cure for a long week is a night at Bloomington's first comedy club. Laughter is the best medicine, after all. This intimate, 164-seat venue on 4th and Walnut has been cheering up Bloomingtonians since 2008. While every table in the house feels close to the brick-backdrop stage, it's best to get there when doors open, particularly if you like to be choosy about a table or if you have friends you want to sit with. The location is close to a variety of restaurants, but it's advised to resist the temptation and arrive hungry, and maybe a little thirsty. A full dinner and drinks menu awaits, and the Electric Root Beer Float, a classic root beer with a shot of whiskey, is kind of a big deal.

123 S Walnut St., 812-336-5233
comedyattic.com

TIP

Laugh for days during the Limestone Comedy Festival, which happens downtown every spring. Check it out at limestonefest.com.

BEAT
YOUR HIGH SCORE
AT THE CADE

If today's video games are a little too "real-looking" for you, take a step back in time and enter the Cade, Bloomington's family-owned retro arcade. Only this place is not for kids; it's for adults 21-plus. That's because the nostalgic game room serves themed cocktails, like the Mario Tart or Gin & Sonic. While sipping on a fun drink, you can take your turn at beating your previous high score. The selection of games offers something for everyone, whether you prefer pinball or board games like Jenga, Yahtzee, or Connect4. It doesn't matter if your strong suit is shooting hoops or avoiding ghosts, it's all fun and games at the Cade.

217 N Walnut St., 812-287-7181
thecade812.com

TIP
Pool and darts more your thing? Head next door to the Video Saloon.

FROLIC
ON THE BIG PIANO
AT THE WONDERLAB MUSEUM

Ever since seeing the 1988 movie *Big*, you've always secretly wanted to dance on a giant floor piano, right? Make your inner child happy and head to the Wonderlab for an afternoon of fun and discovery. After you attempt "Heart and Soul," pull up a seat at the Animation Station and produce a stop-motion flick, test your strength using a pulley chair, create an invisible magnetic field with the MagnetoScope, experiment with electricity, and quench your curiosity with lots more hands-on stations. While this all-ages museum is open year-round, spring and summer are great seasons to visit the outdoor gardens (visible from the B-Line trail), where guests can learn about pollinators, solar power, and composting. What else would you expect from a destination located smack dab in the middle of the Bloomington Entertainment and Arts District?

308 W 4th St., 812-337-1337
wonderlab.org

TIP

Just outside the Wonderlab garden you'll find the Captain Janeway Statue, the *Star Trek: Voyager* character played by Kate Mulgrew. The monument honors all those who were inspired by her role and was placed in Bloomington as a reference to the character's future birthplace.

WATCH SANTA FLIP THE SWITCH
AT THE CANOPY OF LIGHTS

If ever there was a real-life Whoville moment, it would be during the annual Canopy of Lights festival in late November. Seemingly the entire town gathers around the Courthouse Square to sing carols and sip hot chocolate while friendly elves pass out candy canes on every corner. The festivities culminate with Santa taking the stage to lead the crowd in a highly anticipated countdown. After "three, two, one," Santa flips the switch, illuminating thousands of lights draping over downtown. It's a sparkling commencement to the holidays and a wonderful time to get photos with Santa (or drop him a letter) and perhaps do some local gift shopping around the square. Many shops and restaurants remain open to welcome event-goers and share holiday treats.

100 W Kirkwood Ave.
visitbloomington.com/events/annual-events/canopy-of-lights

DANCE IN LINE
AT MIKE'S MUSIC & DANCE BARN

You don't have to be on social media to learn a new group dance. Do it the old-fashioned way! Put on your dancing shoes—or boots—and head to Mike's Music & Dance Barn for a line dancing lesson you won't soon forget. No experience is required, and all ages are welcome. Here you can spread out on the 2,500-square-foot dance floor and learn the steps to some of your favorite songs. Heel, toe, heel, toe . . . you'll be stepping in unison in no time. While the whole family is welcome to learn some new moves and order good food, only those 21-plus can enjoy the bar area. Be sure to check their Facebook page for upcoming events. The venue also hosts live bands and DJs, so you can keep practicing your fancy footwork.

2277 W St. Rd. 46, Nashville, 812-988-8636
facebook.com/mikesdancebarn

SAMPLE MUSIC FROM AROUND THE WORLD
AT LOTUS FESTIVAL

It's no secret that Bloomington is known for its vibrant arts scene, and that includes music. The Lotus World Music & Arts Festival is one of the oldest world music festivals in the US, and it happens every fall on stages throughout downtown. Started by two musicians and a booking agent in 1994, the festival has gained serious momentum over the years and now attracts thousands to explore and discover music from cultures around the world. Several street blocks are closed for event-goers to experience new talent and global genres. There's no wrong way to enjoy the shows, whether you hang at the same venue for an entire evening or bounce around to sample different artists. A schedule of dates, musicians, and venues is posted on the website.

lotusfest.org

PLAY TRIVIA
WITH THE BLOOMINGTON PUB QUIZ

What year did *Game of Thrones* premiere? Do you know who wrote *Jurassic Park*? Which Greek historian is known as the "Father of History"? Test your knowledge of pop culture, sports, geography, food, history, and more when you play team trivia with the Bloomington Pub Quiz. Find the traveling trivia company at local bars, breweries, and restaurants around town. Check their social media to see what nights you can play, then gather your team, come up with a catchy team name, and cash in on your talent for knowing a little about a lot of topics. Many of the pubs that host the Bloomington Pub Quiz offer team prizes or gift cards for your next visit. And in case you're wondering, it's 2011, Michael Crichton, and Herodotus. How did you do?

facebook.com/bloomingtonpubquiz

TIP

If the name-o of your game-o is Bingo, you won't be disappointed to learn several local bars, restaurants, and organizations offer regular game nights. Check out the Upstairs Pub for Music Video Bingo; Switchyard Brewing Company for Music Bingo; or follow Bloomington Bar Bingo on social media for upcoming events.

IMMERSE YOURSELF IN THE ARTS
DURING FIRST THURSDAYS ON CAMPUS

The IU Arts and Humanities Council hosts First Thursday Festivals for many of the months in the school year. It's when the community meets student organizations in a hands-on collaboration to explore the arts and learn about IU's diversity of organizations. Local and student artists invite the public to experience all kinds of new activities, like working with clay, upcycling materials, exploring fashion design, or dancing to a new beat. Enjoy an array of live performances that varies from month to month. Ballet, opera, break dancing—it's all fair game within the Fine Arts Plaza. Festivities go from 5 p.m. to 8 p.m. and generally include food trucks and refreshments, but be sure to check the website for event dates.

The Fine Arts Plaza is located between the Eskenazi Art Museum and the IU Auditorium.

TIP

Public parking is available in the Eagleson Avenue Parking Garage, the Fee Lane Garage, and occasionally in the Indiana Memorial Union lot. Fees may vary.

Lake Monroe
Photo courtesy of Visit Bloomington

SPORTS
AND RECREATION

THROW AXES LIKE A KNIGHT
AT AXECALIBUR

If axe throwing isn't on your radar to try, it should be. At Axecalibur, guests can take aim at one of several targets at this indoor facility on the west side of town. No need for any previous experience, the "axe-perts" will teach you the proper technique to stay safe and have fun. After a few practice throws, engage in an interactive game with digital scoring. Games like Line-Up-Four, Tic-Tac-Toe, and Duck Hunter are among the options. Whether you're solo, with a group, or hosting a special event, the team at Axecalibur is equipped to make sure everyone has an exciting "axe-perience." Walk-ins are welcome, but reservations, especially for groups, are highly recommended. You can also bring your own snacks and non-alcoholic beverages.

3604 W 3rd St., 812-822-1157
axecaliburs.com

TIP

Kids must be at least 12 years old to participate in axe throwing, but for those 5 years and up, there's a GellyBall arena inside! In this thrilling game, kids shoot GellyBall Blasters, a small handheld device that fires soft gel balls. Capture the flag, anyone?

CONQUER
THE CORN MAZE
AT FOWLER PUMPKIN PATCH

Falling leaves and cooler temps can only mean one thing: the Fowler Pumpkin Patch is open. Get ready to take gorgeous fall photos with your favorite autumn activities as the backdrop. Bring the kids for a family hayride, say hello to some adorable goats, shop for fall decor like colorful mums and a variety of gourds, and see if you can conquer the giant corn maze. Some advice: ask for a map and start with the small maze before entering the larger labyrinth. To celebrate your grand exit, grab a wagon and head to the field to select your perfect pumpkins. And for adults 21-plus, check out the beer garden serving seasonal wines and beers. Follow them on social media to see when they open for the season, usually around late September.

5060 N Greene County Line Rd., 812-327-4895
facebook.com/fowlerpumpkinpatch

TIP
For Halloween, don't miss the haunted hayrides during the last week in October.

LUNCH BREAK
NEAR THE WATERFALL
AT LOWER CASCADES PARK

Pack a lunch and head to some of the best picnic tables in town. Located fewer than three miles north of the downtown square, this serene public space is an ideal area to quickly escape the hustle and bustle, even if just for an hour. Several large limestone tables are spread throughout the park, some of which overlook Cascade Creek. The short hike along the boardwalk to the falls is a nice way to reset after lunch before tackling the afternoon. Be sure to come back when you have more time to explore and play. Kids love the massive playground near the entrance, and walkers/joggers enjoy the wide, paved trail that runs the length of the park.

2851 N Old State Rd. 37
Bloomington Parks and Recreation: 812-349-3700
bloomington.in.gov/parks/parks/lower-cascades

TIP

Keep chasing waterfalls at Leonard Springs Nature Park. This moderately rugged 1.1-mile loop on the southwest side of town features two caves, a waterfall, views of the wetlands, and great birdwatching. Find park info at bloomington.in.gov/parks/parks/leonard-springs-nature-park.

STRIKE A POSE
IN FRONT OF THE SAMPLE GATES

The Sample Gates at the intersection of Kirkwood and Indiana is perhaps the most recognizable architectural structure in Bloomington. This impressive entryway to campus is the number one backdrop for graduation pictures, wedding party photos, or visitors and students posing for selfies. The gates stand on the edge of Old Crescent, a group of historic buildings that were part of the original campus when it moved to this location. Plans to build the Gates were presented and rejected multiple times before finally being funded by Edson Sample in 1987 and dedicated to his parents. During the dedication ceremony, then IU President John Ryan said, "The gates stand as a monument to those who have gone before us, to the work and vision of all who've helped to bring this university to greatness."

East Kirkwood and South Indiana Avenues

TIP

Head west on Kirkwood and have a meal or drink at nearby Lennie's. This locally owned restaurant has been a favorite for residents since 1989. While known for its gourmet pizza, Lennie's is also where the Bloomington Brewing Company was born in 1994, making it the first brewpub in southern Indiana. You can also find BBC beer on tap around town. Cheers!

HIKE THE
WOLF CAVE TRAIL
AT MCCORMICK'S CREEK STATE PARK

At McCormick's Creek State Park, hikers traverse through diverse forest trees and wildflowers, pass by scenic waterfalls and sinkholes, and glimpse into cave formations. This is Indiana's first state park, and its rich history can be seen through stunning geological formations including Wolf Cave. The cave was formed as underground water began to carve through the limestone bedrock, forming a network of narrow passageways, nooks, and crannies. To see the cave, take Trail 5, a moderate two-mile loop that circles Wolf Cave Nature Preserve. Why the name Wolf Cave? One legend is that an early settler named Nancy Peden was passing by the cave when wolves emerged. She threw down her bonnet and gloves as a distraction before escaping safely back home. Note: according to the Indiana Department of Natural Resources, there is no breeding population of wolves in Indiana.

250 McCormick's Creek Park Rd., Spencer, 812-829-2235
on.in.gov/mccormickscreeksp

TIP
Some trails may be under repair from storm damage. Call or check the website for updates on trail closures.

EAT YOUR WAY THROUGH
AN EDIBLE COMMUNITY ORCHARD

Enter through the iron gate and discover an enchanting edible orchard near Winslow Woods Park. The Bloomington Community Orchard is a nonprofit group growing fruit trees, berries, and more—all of which are available for anyone to harvest. The orchard is open year-round from sunup to sundown, with summer and early fall being prime times to visit. Find a map of the orchard on their website so you can easily navigate from the apples and pears to the berries and herbs. Or simply meander the grounds and leave feeling inspired, perhaps even curious about honing your own planting and pruning skills. If that's the case, roll up your sleeves and sign up for a free "work and learn" day between April and November. No experience? No problem. A friendly volunteer will show you the ropes.

2120 S Highland Ave.
bloomingtoncommunityorchard.org

LOOK FOR
SANDHILL CRANES
AT GOOSE POND FISH
AND WILDLIFE AREA

Nature lover or not, if it's wintertime, here come the cranes. The spectacular north-bound migration at Goose Pond Fish and Wildlife Area in Greene County is a sight to see, with or without binoculars. Go watch thousands of four-foot-tall sandhill cranes gather across 9,000 acres of wetland to roost and refuel for the remainder of their journey. Among them, look for a very rare and endangered family of whooping cranes—fewer than 700 exist in the wild. Their snow-white feathers and five-foot stature help them stand out in the crowd. Learn all about these impressive creatures and the wetland wildlife at the Visitor Center, which is open year-round. This destination is a regular stop for birders and nature photographers from across the state.

13540 W 400 S, Linton, 812-512-9185
on.in.gov/goosepondfwa

TIP
A great way to experience the cranes is by attending the annual Marsh Madness festival in late February or early March. The festival offers self-guided driving tours, food trucks, activities for kids, and cranes for days.

PIONEER
THROUGH SPRING MILLS STATE PARK

We have the Civilian Conservation Corps (CCC) to thank for much of the restoration of Pioneer Village in Spring Mills State Park. This 1800s village is a carefully preserved settlement offering a glimpse at how early entrepreneurs worked with nature to operate several powerful mills using water flowing from nearby cave streams. Among the establishments in the village, you'll find the apothecary, weaver's shop, blacksmith, distillery, pottery shop, and more. But the main attraction is the three-story limestone gristmill built in 1817. Outside the village, visitors can take a guided boat tour through the Twin Caves and look for endangered blind cavefish. Plan to visit the Nature Center overlooking the lake and explore multiple hiking trails. For overnighting, check out the Spring Mill Inn or reserve one of many campsites.

3333 IN-60 E, Mitchell, 812-849-3534
in.gov/dnr/state-parks/parks-lakes/spring-mill-state-park

GET A VIEW FROM THE TOP
AT THE HICKORY RIDGE LOOKOUT TOWER

Tucked away along the edge of the Charles C. Deam Wilderness Area of the Hoosier National Forest you'll find the last remaining lookout tower of the area jetting into the treetops. Visitors are welcome to climb the 133 metal stairs more than 100 feet to the top cabin. Note: using the handrails is highly recommended. The tower was built in 1939 by the Civilian Conservation Corps and used to watch for fires until the 1970s. Many of the men and women recruited to tower duty were local farmers. During peak fire season, firefighters were stationed to the base, ready to dispatch at a moment's notice, sometimes even four or five times a day. Today, the tower is used for a panoramic glimpse of the surrounding forest. Take State Road 446 south from State Road 46 out of Bloomington and turn left at Tower Ridge Road. The tower is about five miles down on the left.

TIP

Hoosier National Forest is a popular area for mushroom hunting in the spring. Morels are the most popular, but you can also find puffballs and chanterelles. Collecting these mushrooms is only allowed for personal use.

BREAK AWAY
FROM AN ORDINARY SPORTING EVENT AT THE LITTLE 500

Experience the "World's Greatest College Weekend" up close as you cheer on four-person teams cycling around a quarter-mile track at Bill Armstrong Stadium. But first, if you haven't seen the 1979 coming-of-age tale *Breaking Away*, make tonight a movie night. The film takes place in Bloomington, Indiana, and follows a group of local teens through the lens of a fictional character named Dave, who obsesses over cycling. It all culminates with a heated competition at the Little 500, the real-life bike race that started in 1951 to raise money for students working their way through school and has since given more than $2 million to deserving students. Now, every spring, you can experience the pageantry up close when you join the 25,000 fans at the largest collegiate bike race in the United States.

1606 N Fee Ln., 812-855-2794
iusf.indiana.edu/little500

TIP

Ready to put your pedals to the test? Register for the annual Hilly Hundred cycling event that happens every fall. Join a couple thousand riders on an epic two-day adventure featuring live entertainment along the way.

TAKE THE
SEVEN VISTAS CHALLENGE
IN BROWN COUNTY STATE PARK

The best way to experience the 16,000 acres of old-growth forest that make up Brown County State Park is to strike a pose behind each of the wooden frames at all seven vista points. To fully complete the challenge, post your photos using hashtag #BC7VistaChallenge, then stop by the Brown County Visitor Center to claim your gift. Many of the stops are ideal places for a picnic. One of the more popular lookouts is No. 2, Hesitation Point Vista, where on a clear day you can see five miles into the horizon. At Vista No. 5 you'll find a nature center overlooking Strahl Lake Valley. Inside, kids get a kick out of interacting with nature exhibits and saying hello to the critters.

West Gate: 1405 State Rd. 46 W, Nashville
North Gate: 1801 State Rd. 46 E, Nashville
on.in.gov/browncountysp

TIP

Plan to stroll through downtown Nashville where you can pop in and out of shops and galleries, find a spot to dine outdoors, or satisfy a sweet tooth with handmade fudge, ice cream, or an oversized baked good from "Ooey Gooey" Cinnamon Rolls.

WITNESS HOOSIER TRADITIONS
AND LEARN THE WORDS TO "INDIANA, OUR INDIANA"

From tailgating outside Memorial Stadium to joining the crowd in "Sweet Caroline," there's a surplus of collegiate traditions to take part in throughout the year. First, you'll need to learn the words to "Indiana, Our Indiana" and "Hail to Old IU." The fight song and the university's official alma mater song, respectively, are must-knows for Hoosier fans, as are Fists and Blades (check out a YouTube tutorial). Additional customs include the coveted trophies passed back and forth between IU and Purdue for the winner of key rivalry matches. Watch to see who takes home the Golden Boot for women's soccer, the Barn Burner Trophy for women's basketball, the Old Oaken Bucket for football, and the prized Governor's Cup for the overall winner. And don't sleep on women's softball. These ladies bring the heat, along with a roster of catchy cheers.

iuhoosiers.com

TIP

Invest in a pair of candy-striped pants.
As the story goes, legendary IU swim coach
James "Doc" Counsilman and diving coach
Hobie Billingsley outfitted swimmers in the 1960s
with stripes to better see the athletes in the water.
The stripes then made their basketball debut in
1971 as warm-up pants for Bobby Knight's first
Hoosier team, and the rest is history. Today
these iconic stripes are synonymous with
Hoosier fan gear and are literally part of
the fabric of IU culture.

WATCH FOR TRAINS
AT "THE VIADUCT"

Go see one of the longest train trestles in the world still in use. It's located in Greene County, about 20 miles southwest of Bloomington. Visitors can marvel at bridge X75-6, more often called the Tulip Trestle, or "the Viaduct" by locals. Completed in 1906, the railroad bridge stretches more than 2,300 feet across the Richland Creek Valley from 157 feet in the air. And thanks to Tulip Trestle Community Restoration Inc., observers now have a safe space to be awed by the early-1900s engineering. The observation deck was built by community volunteers and has a few noteworthy details of its own. Look for "No. 1504" stamped in concrete in the center. That was the last steam locomotive to cross the trestle. And notice the concrete walkway designed beautifully to mimic the tracks.

County Rd. 480 E, Bloomfield
tuliptrestle.org

TIP

In December, don't miss the Santa Train passing through. On this day, arrive early to have a hot breakfast at the Yoho General Store in Solsberry.

HIKE, PADDLE, FISH, REPEAT
AT GRIFFY LAKE

Try stand-up paddle boarding or take a seat in a kayak or canoe. Griffy Lake Boathouse makes spending a day immersed in nature uber convenient, considering it's only a few miles north of downtown. A series of wooded nature trails will help you get your steps in, and for anglers, the Indiana Department of Natural Resources stocks the lake with bluegill, redear sunfish, largemouth bass, and more. Note: a valid Indiana fishing license is required. While Griffy Lake can sometimes be overshadowed by the ever-popular Lake Monroe, it's worth noting Lake Griffy was the "OG" water source for Bloomington residents. In 1924, Griffy Creek was dammed to create the lake, which kept Bloomingtonians hydrated until the 1950s, when Lake Lemon and later Lake Monroe took over.

3595 N Headley Rd., 812-349-3732
bloomington.in.gov/parks/parks/griffy-lake

TIP
If motorboats are more your speed, boat rentals are available at Lake Lemon Marina and several rental companies along Lake Monroe.

SKATE, PUTT, BOWL,
AND LIVE LIKE A KID AGAIN

If you're a child of the '80s (or close enough), you'll get a kick out of lacing up a pair of roller skates at Western Skateland. The indoor rink offers open skate times for all ages as well as designated times for those 18-plus. Feeling rusty? They also have lessons for kids and adults. If you'd rather keep your sneakers on and practice your putt-putt skills, head over to Hoosier Putt Hole for outdoor miniature golf. Here you'll also find the Tap Hole, a full bar for those 21 and up. And if it's been too long since you've been bowling, the nine lanes within the Indiana Memorial Union on campus are the ultimate Hoosier experience. Or try Classic Lanes, a 32-lane bowling center located about a mile off campus. In addition to a full bar, Classic Lanes also sells snacks and pizza.

TIP

Ready to try figure skating? October through March, Frank Southern Ice Arena is open for public ice skating with the option to rent skates. Call 812-349-3741 for hours and events.

VENUES

Western Skateland
930 W 17th St., 812-332-7288
westernskateland.com

Hoosier Putt Hole and the Tap Hole
4747 State Rd. 46, 812-935-7888
hoosierhole.com

Bowling at Indiana Memorial Union
900 E 7th St., Ste. 3905, 812-855-2328
facebook.com/imubackalley

Classic Lanes
1421 N Willis Dr., 812-332-6689
classiclanesin.com

TEE OFF
WITH A GAME OF DISC GOLF

A college town with beautiful parks and scenery is bound to be a hotspot for disc golf. There are a number of courses in Bloomington and the surrounding area that offer opportunities for beginners and families as well as experienced players and leagues. If you're unfamiliar with the game, think frisbee meets golf. Players take turns throwing discs along a 9-, 18-, or even 24-hole course until the discs land in the basket for that hole. As in golf, there are even different types of discs depending on the distance you need to throw. The object is to complete the hole in as few throws as possible. The Bloomington Disc Golf Club is a great resource for anyone interested in learning more about public courses and how to get started.

Bloomington Disc Golf Club
bdgc.org

PLAY PICKLEBALL
IN THE PARK

Say that three times fast, then grab your paddles and head to Switchyard Park. Pickleball is the happy medium between tennis and table tennis, with dedicated courts at the north end of the park. In 2019, the 65-acre park that was once an abandoned railroad was officially revealed to the public. Today, the park includes a large pavilion, a picnic shelter, a splash pad, a main stage, two dog parks, bocce ball courts, a basketball court, more than 600 native trees, community garden beds, a skate park, and the newly popular pickleball courts. Players may use the courts on a first-come, first-served basis. There's parking available courtside, but if you're feeling extra energetic, you can bike or walk the B-Line trail that runs alongside the courts and through the entirety of the park. If the courts are in use, try one of the six outdoor courts at RCA Community Park.

Switchyard Park	RCA Park
1601 S Rogers St.	1400 W RCA Park Dr.

TIP

Bloomington Parks & Recreation hosts a number of fun events year-round, like adult field days, live concerts, outdoor movies, and more. Follow them on social media or pick up a hard copy program guide at City Hall.

DIG FOR FOSSILS
AT LAKE MONROE

Lots of cool fossils can be found along the trails and shores of Lake Monroe, but you're not allowed to collect them. Unless . . . you head to the fossil dig area at the Paynetown State Recreation Area and look for the large wooden bed full of Waldron Shale. It's a fossiliferous layer of rock containing common fossils. A helpful identification chart is on the nearby sign, along with information about the rock's origins. Inside the pit, you can collect brachiopod shells, crinoid bodies, snails, trilobites, corals, and an occasional clam shell. It's a real-life treasure hunt, especially if you strike it rich with pyrite, otherwise known as "fool's gold." Bonus if you go after it rains, when the fossils become more exposed from the surface. So check the weather and plan accordingly. Happy fossil hunting.

4850 S State Rd. 446, 812-837-9546
on.in.gov/monroelake

TIP

Just south of the Paynetown State Recreation Area is the Amy Weingartner Branigin Peninsula Preserve located off Rush Ridge Road. This 2.2-mile out-and-back trail offers breathtaking views of Lake Monroe on either side. Note: this Sycamore Land Trust property is closed on weekends and holidays to help prevent heavy use.

SOAR
UP, UP, AND AWAY
IN A HOT AIR BALLOON

Look for your neighborhood from above the treeline while getting a bird's-eye view of scenic Bloomington. There's a reason so many folks have a hot air balloon ride on their bucket list—it's an exhilarating way to see the sights from a new point of view. According to one pilot, the best time to book a flight is during peak fall foliage, around mid- to late-October, but spring and even winter are becoming more popular times to soar. Many Bloomington companies in the area offer sunrise or sunset trips that often end with a champagne toast. If you'd rather watch with your feet on the ground, or go up in a tethered balloon, the Kiwanis Hot Air Balloon Festival in fall offers rides, spectacular shows, and a chance to see the balloons up close.

Balloons Over Bloomington
2700 S Kirby Rd., 812-345-9598
balloonsoverbloomington.com

SkyVista Ballooning
1370 W That Rd., 812-369-5732
skyvistaballooning.com

TJV Balloons
5780 N Bottom Rd., 812-320-0966
tjvballoons.com

STOP AND ARRANGE THE FLOWERS
AT THE SEEDLINGS

Have you ever been curious about the technique and design elements that go into arranging a stunning bouquet, wreath, or centerpiece? Sign up for a workshop at the Seedlings Flower Truck and learn from a passionate flower farmer and former teacher. With the help of her husband, kids, and extended family, owner Laura Deck launched a unique business that allows customers to channel their inner artist and connect with nature. Not only does she host classes on the farm, she also takes their business on the road, hence the "truck." After her family converted an old Chevy, the Seedlings Flower Truck now travels to on-site events, where they conduct DIY bouquet building for weddings, office parties, and graduations. Additionally, she offers U-pick events during the summer months.

6575 N Bottom Rd., 812-369-0049
theseedlingsflowertruck.com

VENTURE OVER THE WATER AND THROUGH THE WOODS
AT YELLOWWOOD STATE FOREST

You might not be heading to Grandmother's, but you'll certainly be trekking over water and through the woodlands when you hike the Lake Trail at Yellowwood State Forest, located about 10 miles east of Bloomington. The 4.5-mile trail takes visitors on a loop around Yellowwood Lake, a 133-acre body of water completed by the Civilian Conservation Corps and Works Project Administration in 1939. Depending on the year, you may even see the namesake yellowwood tree in bloom. Its small, fragrant, white flowers make an appearance every three to five years in the spring. The forest is also home to a large population of neotropical migratory birds like scarlet tanagers and cerulean warblers, so bring your binoculars and field guides.

772 S Yellowwood Rd., Nashville, 812-988-7945
on.in.gov/yellowwoodsf

TIP

Up for a little road trip? While in Nashville, visit two historic covered bridges. The 1880 Bean Blossom Covered Bridge spans the Bean Blossom Creek on Covered Bridge Road. From there, head south to the north entrance of Brown County State Park, where you'll find the 1838 double-tunneled Ramp Creek Covered Bridge.

CLIMB TO THE TOP
AT HOOSIER HEIGHTS

Satisfy your curiosity about rock climbing in the comfort of an indoor gym. Beginners, fear not, no experience is required to work your way to the top—just a willingness to learn. A team of experts is there to literally show you the ropes. First-timers get a staff-led tour and in-depth orientation on how to use the gear and different types of climbing systems. The gym offers bouldering, top ropes, auto belays, lead climbing, and more, all of which newcomers learn about on day one. Adding to the experience, parts of the gym are located inside an old historic church with lots of natural lighting and open spaces. Yoga and fitness classes are also available, as well as events and youth programs.

1008 S Rogers St., 812-824-6414
hoosierheightsbloomington.com

TIP
Hoosier Heights sells a variety of climbing shoes and gear in addition to offering rentals.

CHANNEL YOUR INNER SHERLOCK HOLMES
TO ESCAPE THE ROOM

Invite a few friends, family members, or co-workers and test your group's inner sleuthing abilities. At Code and Key Escape Rooms inside Fountain Square Mall, parties of two or more (four to six is ideal) work together to crack the code in a variety of indoor or even outdoor settings, like DaVinci's Workshop and the Stolen Artifact. Or, at Hoosier Escape House, less than a mile north of the Square, you become a group of thieves in a high-stakes casino heist. In another scenario you're working with fellow "inmates" to break out of prison and hurry to the getaway car before the guards come back. With so many adventures to choose from at either escape room company, you're promised to have a thrilling experience.

Hoosier Escape House
933 N Walnut St., 812-822-0639
hoosierescapehouse.com

The Code and Key Escape Rooms
101 W Kirkwood Ave., Ste. 113, 812-214-1497
codeandkeyescaperooms.com

SMELL RARE BLOOMS
IN THE BIOLOGY BUILDING GREENHOUSE

In 2016, thousands of visitors stood in line to catch a glimpse—or whiff—of the rare corpse flower housed inside the Biology Building Greenhouse. The plant, nicknamed "Wally," blooms once every few years and is among more than 800 species of desert, rainforest, and carnivorous plants inside the always-warm greenhouse. Each of the conservatory rooms is packed with unique and diverse plants, like the chocolate tree in Room J or the pineapple plant and welwitschia in Room A. The latter only produces two leaves, which can grow up to 13 feet long. In Room F, you'll find bug-eating plants like the venus flytrap and the tropical pitcher plant. The greenhouse is free to visit and open to the public during select times. Check their website for current hours and important reminders for visitors.

1001 E 3rd. St., 812-855-7717
greenhouse.biology.indiana.edu

TIP

Take advantage of another rare opportunity on campus when you visit the Kirkwood Observatory, which is open to the public on select evenings. Visitors can look through a 12-inch refractor telescope to see planets, star clusters, and the moon. Find details at astro.indiana.edu/outreach/kirkwood-observatory.

THROW CLAY
AT POTTERY HOUSE STUDIO

Get your hands on a new hobby or expand your current love of pottery when you sign up for a class at Pottery House Studio. Attendees of the adult classes learn the basics of centering and throwing clay on a pottery wheel while also learning how to hand-build sculptures and shapes from a slab. Top it off with a few key decorating techniques and you'll be making your own functional works of art in just a few weeks. Not ready to get your hands in the clay? Choose from a large selection of pre-made pottery you can paint at home or in the studio, or grab a to-go kit, with all the tools you need to work with clay at home.

223 S Pete Ellis Dr., Ste. 17, 812-650-2884
potteryhousestudio.com

TIP

If it's the weekend, head to Piccoli Dolci in suite 27. Inside this sweet pop-up shop, you'll find authentic Italian cookies, pastries, and savory treats, in case you miss them at the Woolery Farmers Market. Check their website for hours at piccolidolci.net.

GO BIRDING
AT BEANBLOSSOM BOTTOMS NATURE PRESERVE

Grab your binoculars and rubber boots and head to Beanblossom Bottoms Nature Preserve, located northwest of town. From the small gravel parking lot you'll discover a 2.5-mile mostly boardwalk trail snaking barely above the wetlands. The habitat is ideal for seeing many varieties of birds year-round, including seven species of woodpecker. Look for the pileated, hairy, downy, red-bellied, and red-headed woodpeckers, as well as yellow-bellied sapsuckers and northern flickers (also woodpeckers). In summer you might even catch a glimpse of a colorful prothonotary warbler. Beanblossom Bottoms Nature Preserve has been designated a state Important Bird Area by the National Audubon Society and a Wetland of Distinction by the Society of Wetland Scientists. The more than 700 acres are protected by the Sycamore Land Trust.

N Woodall Rd., Ellettsville
sycamorelandtrust.org/preserves/beanblossom-bottoms-nature-preserve

TIP
Stop by Wild Birds Unlimited nature shop on your way and pick up a handy field guide to help you identify birds in the area.

TAG! HAVE A BLAST
AT LASERLITE

Think laser tag is just for kids? Think again, and get ready for a fast-paced activity for all ages. At LaserLite, players get all the equipment and instructions they need to safely compete against their opponents in a large indoor arena. Fun obstacles and dimly glowing lights set the scene for competitive play. It's no surprise this is a popular destination for work outings, special events, rainy days, and birthdays, whether you're celebrating 8 or 40. If members of your group aren't interested in laser tag, there's an extensive arcade with both classic and modern games. Pizza and soft drinks are also available on site. Check their website for weekly game specials or to book a private event. May the best team win.

4505 E 3rd St., 812-337-0456
lasertagandfun.com

TIP

There's more fun and games to be played every summer during the Monroe County Fair, where visitors can try outdoor laser tag on the north lawn. Check out monroecountyfairgrounds.

KID-FRIENDLY INDOOR ACTIVITIES

Urban Air Adventure Park
More than an indoor trampoline park, kids
can soar, climb, and complete obstacle courses.
3603 W State Rd. 46, 812-727-8309
urbanair.com/indiana-bloomington

Jump-N-Joeys
Jump around in a variety of large bounce
houses and win fun prizes in the arcade.
108 N Curry Pike, 812-822-1947
jumpatjoeys.com

The Warehouse
Littles love the large playground while older
kids enjoy the skatepark, climbing wall, and more.
1525 S Rogers St., 812-333-3951
btownwarehouse.com

MAKE A SPLASH
AT THE IU OUTDOOR POOL

On warm summer days, the Indiana University outdoor pool is the place to cool off. With a day pass or 30-day membership, visitors can chill in the main pool, lounge on an expansive deck, make a splash off the diving board in a separate diving well, or get a workout in the 50-meter lap lanes. There are also concessions with a variety of snacks and drinks. Not quite comfortable with your or your family's swim skills? The pool hosts swim lessons for kids and adults throughout the summer. An especially fun treat is when they host Dive-In Movie Nights. The pool stays open extra late into the evening to show a movie on the big screen while guests enjoy a late-night swim.

1490 N Fee Ln., 812-855-9584
outdoorpool.indiana.edu

TIP
Families can also cool off at Bryan Park Pool or Mill's Pool, operated by the City of Bloomington Parks and Recreation. Every year, toward the end of summer, Mill's Pool hosts a special pool paw-ty just for doggies. Check out Drool in the Pool at bloomington.in.gov/parks/events/drool-in-pool.

POSE WITH A GOAT
AT THE GOAT CONSPIRACY

Heading east from Bloomington toward Nashville you'll find a charming farm and creamery called the Goat Conspiracy. And yes, they offer goat yoga during the warmer months. Visitors can also reserve a farm tour and spend time taking selfies with these quirky creatures, all while learning how they interact with the free-range chickens and surrounding land. The farm is run by a small but mighty crew, including a resident cheesemaker who produces several styles of fresh goat cheeses, as well as a variety of goat milk soaps, which can be ordered online. For overnight guests or future getaways, the property also includes a beautiful country cabin that sleeps eight. Because this is a working farm, the owners ask that guests book an experience online ahead of time.

6022 E Kent Rd., 812-322-2879
thegoatconspiracy.com

TIP
The farm also offers soap making workshops. Participants learn the basics and bring home a handful of small-batch artisan soaps. Check the website for upcoming classes.

First Friday Gallery Walk

CULTURE
AND HISTORY

SEE THE WORLD'S LARGEST PUZZLE COLLECTION
AT LILLY LIBRARY

Take a trip to IU's rare books and manuscripts library, where you'll find hundreds of thousands of rare books and millions of manuscripts. A New Testament of the Gutenberg Bible might be the most extraordinary item among Lilly Library's rarities, but not to be overshadowed is the Jerry Slocum Collection, an impressive assemblage of 35,000 mechanical puzzles—some of which are on display for patrons to solve. Not to be confused with jigsaw or word puzzles, mechanical puzzles need to be manipulated to figure out (think Rubik's Cube). According to Andrew Rhoda, Curator of Puzzles at Lilly, patrons can request books from Mr. Slocum's collection, including the books on puzzle design. They can also request to see materials from the Slocum manuscript collection, which includes Mr. Slocum's correspondence with puzzle designers and other puzzle collectors.

1200 E 7th St., 812-855-2452
libraries.indiana.edu/lilly-library

TIP

Also on display at Lilly Library are golden Oscars won by legendary film director John Ford, who directed *The Informer* and *The Grapes of Wrath*. Curious what it's like to hold an Oscar? All you need is an appointment with the library.

TAKE A GUIDED LOOK BACK IN TIME
AT T. C. STEELE

If you've made the trip from Bloomington to Brown County, you've likely breezed by the T. C. Steele State Historic Site, where famed impressionist painter T. C. Steele and his wife Selma purchased land in 1907. Here they established their home, named "The House of Singing Winds," alongside Steele's art studio and Selma's sprawling picture-perfect (or painting-perfect) gardens. Not long after they moved in, their presence on the hillside drew in more artists, and the Art Colony of the Midwest was born. Today, visitors can take a guided tour of the home and studio, also referred to as "not a gallery," where many of the original artifacts remain. If you're a nature lover, plan to spend extra time hiking five mapped-out trails winding throughout the 211-acre property.

4220 T C Steele Rd., Nashville
indianamuseum.org/historic-sites/tc-steele

WAKE UP EARLY AND GET IN LINE
TO PICK A GLASS PUMPKIN

Cinderella's glass slipper ain't got nothin' on the Bloomington Creative Glass Center's (BCGC) pumpkins. Every year in mid-October, volunteers for this nonprofit educational art center scatter more than 1,000 original glass-blown pumpkins throughout the courthouse lawn. At the strike of 10 a.m., the first person in the line snaking around the square is admitted to select their perfect pumpkin. Pumpkin prices range between $25 and $200. People come from all over the state to snag a spot in line, so pack your coffee and go early. Curious about trying glass blowing? The Center offers classes for anyone with an interest, regardless of age or experience. For a longer-term commitment, check out their apprenticeship program.

100 W Kirkwood Ave.
bloomingtoncreativeglasscenter.org/events/ggpp.html

TIP
Not interested in waiting in line? Join the team of volunteers and get access to the pumpkin of your dreams.

SAY HELLO TO MONROE
AT MONROE COUNTY HISTORY CENTER

Catch a glimpse of the county the way it was during its pioneer days, or the way it was just a few short decades ago. The Monroe County History Center is home to an original 1840s pioneer cabin and gobs of athletic artifacts from IU legends. The best advice is to come often. According to the Center's director, Daniel Schlegel Jr., exhibits are frequently rotating, even within permanent displays. The limestone collection you saw several months ago may be very different today, as precious relics take turns sharing the spotlight. Be sure to say hello to Monroe, the 1,200-pound Kodiak bear, once a towering centerpiece at Schmalz's Department Store until it closed in 1988. And if you see Daniel, ask him about his experience riding a penny-farthing (high wheel) bicycle.

202 E 6th St., 812-332-2517
monroehistory.org

TIP

Take a deep dive into Bloomington's rich history when you attend a Monroe County History Club speaker series event. Programs are free and open to the public. Join their Facebook group to see upcoming programs.

GIVE A HOOT
AND FIND ALL 12 LIMESTONE OWLS ON CAMPUS

Indiana University's Gothic-style beauty can be appreciated with the added challenge of finding all 12 limestone owls on campus. Hint: one of them is not so conspicuous. Look for it atop the largest student union building in the world. Of course, Bloomingtonians are no strangers to limestone. The first limestone quarry was opened in 1827 by Richard Gilbert and has been used to construct iconic buildings ever since. Because limestone is a freestone, meaning it has no preferred place to split, it can meet the demands of most architectural designs and be carved into detailed works of art. Indiana limestone has been used on the Pentagon, the National Cathedral, and the Empire State Building. As for the owls, it's unclear why this particular parliament was chosen, but some speculate it has to do with their symbolism of wisdom and education.

Indiana Memorial Union
900 E 7th St., 812-856-6381
imu.indiana.edu

SPOT ART IN THE FOREST
AT THE SCULPTURE TRAILS
OUTDOOR MUSEUM

About 20 miles west of Bloomington, deep in the woods of Solsberry, explorers will enjoy finding wondrous works of art at the Sculpture Trails Outdoor Museum. Founded in 2002, this fresh-air experience has grown to include more than 150 sculptures along more than three miles of hiking trails. Artists from all over the world have displayed works here for curious adventurers. The park is free and open to the public seven days a week, or reservations for group guided tours can be made in advance. The museum also hosts a series of workshops that teach participants how to do metal casting, make cast iron sculptures, or learn forging techniques using modern and traditional tools for blacksmithing.

6764 N Tree Farm Rd., Solsberry, 505-554-1788
sculpturetrails.com

WALK CLOCKWISE AROUND THE TRAIL
AT THE TIBETAN MONGOLIAN BUDDHIST CENTER

In nearly 100 acres of woods in the southwest corner of Bloomington, visitors can explore the spiritual grounds of the Tibetan Mongolian Buddhist Cultural Center. The center was established in 1979 by the eldest brother of the Dalai Lama, Thubten Norbu, a former professor of Tibetan studies at Indiana University. Near the entrance to the center, you can follow the Kora Nature Meditation Trail through the grounds to explore prayer wheels, monuments, and more. While hikers are free to enjoy the trail in any direction, the tradition is to take the trail clockwise as well as walk clockwise around several Buddhist monuments on the grounds. The center offers tours for a more in-depth experience, as well as many other ways to participate in learning more about the culture.

3655 S Snoddy Rd., 812-336-6807
tmbcc.org

TAKE A HAUNTED WALK IN THE WOODS
TO STEPP CEMETERY

Deep in the middle of Morgan-Monroe State Forest lies Stepp Cemetery, infamously haunted by the woman in black. Many versions of the legend that spooks visitors in this neck of the woods have been told over the years, but they all share the same eerie undertone. It goes something like this: The woman's young child, called Baby Lester, died tragically, followed by the woman herself, and they were both buried in the cemetery. The ghost of the woman would sit on a nearby tree stump, called "the Warlock's Chair," where she would mourn her child. The chair was said to be cursed and anyone who sat on it would also be cursed. The stories swirled through the '50s, '60s, and '70s, and today remain etched in stone, or rather, etched in gravestones.

on.in.gov/morganmonroesf

TIP
Stepp cemetery is located near the Three Lakes Trail and the Walls shelter house, just off Main Forest Road in Morgan-Monroe State Forest.

FIND YOUR MUSE
AT ESKENAZI MUSEUM

Spend a day surrounded by art and artifacts at the Sidney and Lois Eskenazi Museum of Art located on IU's campus. Fun fact: the building was designed by I. M. Pei, the same architect who created the glass pyramid that graces the Louvre in Paris. Now home to more than 45,000 works of art representing cultures throughout time, it's the kind of place you'll want to visit over and over again. Among seven galleries, you can explore everything from ancient gold to art by Picasso and Monet. A piece of advice: check the museum's online event calendar and sign up for a docent-guided experience. It doesn't matter if it's your first time in an art museum or it's a frequent stop, their tours are a welcoming way to interact with experts and learn more about the collections. Who knows, you may even find your muse.

1133 E 7th St., 812-855-5445
artmuseum.indiana.edu

TIP

Squirrel! While you're on campus, head to Dunn's Woods and watch the squirrels in action. Bonus points if you snap an artistic picture for the Squirrels at IU Instagram page, which has thousands of followers and counting.

LEVEL UP
YOUR DIGITAL SKILLS
AT THE MONROE COUNTY
PUBLIC LIBRARY

Have an idea for a podcast? What about a song or short film? Learn the skills to bring your concepts to fruition in the Level Up Digital Creativity Center located on the first floor of the main library. Check the library's calendar for workshops, ranging from graphic design to 3D printing, and then reserve one of four digital creativity workstations to start crafting your masterpiece. Workstations include a variety of software programs for video and animation, audio recording, producing music, coding, and more. There's also a production studio complete with a green screen and two audio production studios. Or, if you simply want to safeguard hard-copy family photos and videos, Level Up even has a memory preservation station for converting these keepsakes into a digital format.

303 E Kirkwood Ave., 812-349-3050
mcpl.info

RAISE A GLASS TO THE ARTS
DURING FIRST FRIDAYS

If it's the first Friday of the month, head downtown for the Gallery Walk. Pop in and out of more than a dozen galleries within a one-mile stretch expanding from 4th and Rogers to campus. A good place to start is Pictura Gallery inside the FAR Center for Contemporary Arts. Nature lovers will especially appreciate a stop at Juniper Art Gallery, where fine art meets fun and approachable gifts. Each participating space stays open from 5 p.m. to 8 p.m. to exhibit distinctive works ranging from photography to painting, sculpture, pottery, glass work, fiber arts, printmaking, and more. Download the map from Gallery Walk's website and explore at your own pace while you mingle with gallery owners and guest artists. Many of the stops include cash bars for beer, wine, and other refreshments.

gallerywalkbloomington.com

TIP
Keep the artistry theme going and make a reservation at Bloomington's eclectically decorated Farm restaurant, located within walking distance of participating art galleries.

MEANDER WITH LOCAL ART LOVERS
AT THE 4TH STREET FESTIVAL

Plan to stay in B-Town for Labor Day and join the crowd of townies, out-of-towners, and new and returning students at the 4th Street Festival of the Arts and Crafts. During the two-day event, a portion of 4th Street is closed to traffic while more than 100 artisans offer their work to passersby. The annual show was founded in 1977 by local artists and is now a nonprofit organization committed to creating a welcoming atmosphere for all to appreciate the works of others. Enjoy musical performances, spoken word, and more taking place at several surrounding stages. Additionally, nearby shops and restaurants are open for visitors to soak in all the Bloomington vibes. If you stay late into the day, treat yourself to dinner at one of 4th Street's numerous international restaurants.

4th Street between Grant Street and Indiana Avenue, 812-575-0484
4thstreet.org

PEEK INSIDE THE HOME OF INDIANA UNIVERSITY'S FIRST PRESIDENT
AT WYLIE HOUSE MUSEUM

After accepting the job as Indiana University's first president, Andrew Wylie moved to Bloomington with his family in 1829. In 1835, he built the two-story brick home that stands on East 2nd Street, just southwest of campus. Years after his death, the home was modernized to reflect a more contemporary style for the time. But in the 1960s, the house was restored to its original design—complete with a collection of artifacts and letters from the Wylie family—and is now owned and managed by Indiana University Libraries as a historic museum. Visitors can take free tours and get a glimpse at what life was like for Wylie, who lived there with his wife and 10 of 12 children who resided there in various numbers over the years. Can't make it just yet? Check out the virtual tour on the Wylie House Museum website.

307 E 2nd St., 812-855-6224
libraries.indiana.edu/wylie-house-museum

Shops and restaurants on
East Kirkwood Avenue.

SHOPPING
AND FASHION

SHOP 'TIL YOU DROP
IN DOWNTOWN BLOOMINGTON

Treat yourself to a shopping spree with plenty of options for breakfast, lunch, and dinner breaks, plus stops for coffee or something stronger, too. It's all within walking distance around the Monroe County Courthouse Square. See what's new inside dozens of local shops, which include vintage clothing, outdoor gear, cookware, books, candles, pottery, and Fair Trade handmade art from around the world. On the south side of the Square, pop into Fountain Square for even more boutique shopping and galleries. When hunger hits, you'll find options for Mexican, Italian, Middle Eastern, Indian, Cajun, American, and more. And if you really want to shop 'til you drop, head east along Kirkwood toward the iconic IU Sample Gates for even more shops and restaurants, with an emphasis on IU gear as you approach campus.

Monroe County Courthouse Square
The courthouse is located at 100 W Kirkwood Ave.
downtownbloomington.com

TIP

Trick or treat! Each year around Halloween, families are invited to the Downtown Bloomington Trick or Treat Walk around the Square. It's a festive occasion for all as local shop owners and staff dress up in costumes to pass out candy to kids and families. Many of the businesses stay open late to cater to fall shoppers and diners.

BUY A SHARE, DONATE A SHARE
AT THE FARMERS MARKET

Every Saturday morning (plus Tuesday evenings in summer), rain, snow, or shine, residents gather at farmers markets throughout town to stock up on locally grown produce, artisanal cheeses, fresh eggs, handmade soaps, chocolate-filled pastries, and more. Plan to linger for live music, say hello to neighbors and friendly pups, and indulge in savory fixings from a food truck or two. Before you leave, pick up a fresh bouquet for the week. It's all part of Bloomington's quintessential buy-local spirit. And one market in particular is taking this community-supported ethos to the next level. Thanks to the People's Cooperative Market's online presence, you can sponsor a farm share for a family in need by visiting peoplesmarketbtown.org.

TIP

Missed the market? Head to Rose Hill Farm Stop or Bloomingfoods. Both co-ops are open daily and have a nice selection of fresh produce, baked goods, honey, teas, coffees, and more—all from local and regional producers, like an Italian favorite, Piccoli Dolci.

FIND YOUR MARKET

Community Farmers Market
April–November; 401 N Morton St.
bloomington.in.gov/farmers-market

Peoples Market
Winter and summer; 2420 E 3rd St.
peoplesmarketbtown.org

Smithville Farmers Market
May–September; 7555 S Strain Ridge Rd.
facebook.com/smithvilleindianafarmersmarket

Tuesday Market
June–September; 1611 S Rogers St.
bloomington.in.gov/farmers-market/tuesday

Winter Farmers Market
November–March; 1603 S Rogers St.
bloomingtonwinterfarmersmarket.com

Woolery Market
April–September; 2250 W Sunstone Dr.
bloomingtonwinterfarmersmarket.com/woolery-farmers-market

ENGAGE IN CHILD'S PLAY
AT MAIRZY DOATS BOOKS & TOYS

Watch a youngster light up with joy when they walk into a local toy shop just for them. Designed for kids to engage, craft, and play with toys and games, Mairzy Doats is the perfect place to find a new screen-free activity while the youngsters are in tow. The store carries gifts for kids of all ages, from plush animals to pretend play sets, crafting kits, and build-it-yourself models. You'll also find a selection of family games and puzzles and a diverse collection of second-hand books. Does the term "Mairzy Doats" sound familiar to you? You might recognize it from the '40s song by The Merry Macs. Its whimsical, playful lyrics are an adorably accurate representation of the store's ambience.

919 S College Mall Rd., 812-822-1686
shopmairzydoats.com

CONNECT
WITH THE COMMUNITY
AT MORGENSTERN'S BOOKS

Who doesn't love a good sequel? The comeback story of Morgenstern's is possibly one of Bloomington's best retakes. This beloved neighborhood bookstore closed in 1996 after the competition among booksellers saturated Bloomington, not to mention the tug-of-war between online markets and independent storefronts. But as years went by, the brick-and-mortar bookstores moved out of town, leaving Bloomingtonians without the kind of place where you can cozy up with a cup of tea, meet up with a book club, or attend an author talk and signing. Enter Morgenstern's, to the rescue! After re-opening in 2021, Morgenstern's Books successfully became Indiana's largest independent bookstore. With a robust children's section, a colorful array of local merch, a cozy cafe, and a packed schedule of in-store events, Morgenstern's is truly a gathering place for the community.

849 S Auto Mall Rd., 812-676-7323
morgensternbooks.com

TIP
Peruse two more beloved independent bookstores located on the Courthouse Square. Pop into the Book Corner for best sellers, classics, puzzles, and children's toys. For rare and used books, immerse yourself in the aisles at Caveat Emptor.

FEED THE BIRDS IN YOUR BACKYARD
AT WILD BIRDS UNLIMITED

Full disclosure: my husband and I own this nature shop; we are huge bird nerds and advocates for nature. Inside the store you'll find everything you need to get started or continue the hobby of backyard bird feeding. The staff especially loves to help beginners with tutorials and recommendations, from feeders that cling to apartment windows to customizable pole- or deck-mount systems. Plus, learn about the different varieties of bird seed and food to attract different types of local birds, like bluebirds, cardinals, chickadees, and more. Follow the store on Facebook for community events, like live raptor demonstrations or how to care for nest boxes during the spring and summer nesting season. Gift shoppers are in for a treat, too, as the store has a selection of books, mugs, candles, wine pourers, art, and more.

1301 S College Mall Rd., 812-369-4255
wbu.com/bloomington

TIP

Take a walk on the wild side with IndiGO Birding Nature Tours. Join fellow birdwatchers for an adventure on foot or by kayak at nearby birding hotspots. David Rupp also takes small groups to Belize to visit a wide range of habitats, often with the goal of seeing 250 or more species. These tours fill up fast, so be sure to check indigobirding.com.

SHOW YOUR HOO, HOO, HOO, HOOSIER PRIDE
IN CREAM & CRIMSON

Whether you're a longtime local, new resident, or just visiting, Hoosier gear is basically a requirement for stepping foot in Bloomington. Indiana University's famous IU interlocking logo, called the trident, can be found on apparel throughout town. But for one of the largest selections, head straight to the source. Inside the Indiana Memorial Union, you'll find the campus bookstore, where you can stock up on everything from shirts and sweatshirts to pet accessories and home decor—all in cream and crimson, of course. But these two specific colors haven't always been the official shades. Records show that in 1887, the university colors were crimson and black, and for the senior class, they were cream and gold. Later the university simplified the colors to red and white but reverted to cream and crimson in 2002.

900 E 7th St., 812-215-8804

TIP
Hungry for an IU-themed meal? Order the award-winning Cream & Crimson Pizza from Aver's Gourmet Pizza.

SHOP FOR IU GEAR

Indiana Hoosiers Team Store (on campus)
Bloomington's headquarters
for Cream and Crimson.
Carmichael Center: 530 E Kirkwood Ave.
Simon Skjodt Assembly Hall: 1001 E 17th St.

Greetings
Trendy game day apparel and sassy gifts.
429 E Kirkwood Ave., 812-332-2737

The Indiana Shop
All things Hoosier gear, including
Adidas candy-striped pants.
421 E Kirkwood Ave., 812-333-1301
1302 E 3rd St., 812-332-3306

SLCT
Curated vintage clothing with '80s and '90s vibes.
208 N Walnut St., slcstock.com

Tracks
IU gear plus a collection of vinyl and CDs.
415 E Kirkwood Ave., 812-332-3576

ROLL THE DICE
AT BLOOMINGTON'S
BOARD GAME SHOPS

It's all fun and games when you visit the Common Room or the Game Preserve. For families, friend groups, parties, and card nights, you'll discover an assortment of clever and curious board game options for any occasion. Each of these hobby shops caters to both experienced players and newbies alike, and each offers a welcoming space for interested gamers to try new games, get recommendations, connect with like-minded game lovers, and buy a fun new game to take home or play in the store. With an extensive selection of novelty games, strategy games, and roleplaying games, plus all the accessories, you just might find a new favorite. Check each store's website for events and organized play opportunities and get ready to take a chance on fun.

The Common Room
223 S Pete Ellis Dr.
812-333-GAME (4263)
commonroomgames.com

The Game Preserve
2894 E 3rd St., Ste. 108
812-332-6602
gamepreserve.com

TIP
Is card collecting more your thing? Visit Hi5 Cards and Collectibles for sports and Pokemon cards. They have graded and raw cards as well as sealed items.

FEEL THE SPIRIT OF THE SOUTHWEST
AT NOT JUST RUGS

It's rare to find authentic Navajo art east of the Mississippi, but if you travel a few blocks north of the Courthouse Square, you'll discover Not Just Rugs, a shop blanketed with art bought directly from Native American tribes in the Southwest. Inside, you'll be greeted with intricate Navajo patterns hand-woven into beautiful rugs. Ask owners Chuck and Andrea about the designs and learn more about the culture from which they originated. For many years, the couple lived on the Navajo reservation in Arizona, where Chuck worked at the Hubbell Trading Post and Andrea taught school. They frequently travel back to purchase art for the gallery, which is more than just rugs, as the name implies. Find woven baskets, jewelry, collectibles, dream catchers, and more.

1117 N College Ave., Ste. D, 812-332-6434
notjustrugs.com

SAMPLE YOUR WAY
THROUGH THE OLIVE LEAF
(PLUS, THERE'S CHOCOLATE!)

At the Olive Leaf on the east side of town, shoppers can sample dozens of fresh olive oils and aged balsamic vinegars, like blood orange–fused olive oil and blackberry ginger balsamic vinegar. The staff is there to guide your experience and help you find the perfect combination, plus a few new recipe ideas, too. Caprese salads will never be the same. And have you ever tried dark chocolate balsamic whipped cream? The shop is also home to the Bloomington Chocolate Company, which is responsible for the sweet, tempting aroma of dessert. Find gourmet truffles, handmade BloomingOs (house dipped sandwich cookies), and giant fancy marshmallows. It's truly a foodie's paradise and a great place to find a gift everyone will enjoy tasting.

2506 E 3rd St., 812-323-3073
oliveleafbloomington.com

TIP

Another sweet spot for chocolate lovers is BLU Boy Chocolate on E Kirkwood. Shop in store or online (bluboystore.com) for locally made gourmet treats.

BAM! EXPLORE ALL THREE FLOORS
OF THE BLOOMINGTON ANTIQUE MALL

Located within the West Side National Historic District and conveniently just off the B-Line trail, the Bloomington Antique Mall (BAM) awaits eager treasure hunters. Inside this three-story, climate-controlled building (which proudly claims to be fully ADA compliant), you'll find unique collectables, vintage decor, antique furniture, and more. There are dozens of booths showcasing diverse and funky items you won't find anywhere else. Whether you're a collector, bargain hunter, or browser, plan to spend a while moving from floor to floor to peruse more than 100 vendors, and plan to visit again soon. It's nearly impossible to see everything in one stop. And if you're making a weekend out of it, check out their sister location, the Exit 76 Antique Mall in Edinburgh, Indiana.

311 W 7th St., 812-323-7676
bloomingtonantiquemall.com

FOCUS ON DOING GREAT
AT BADKNEES

Few things say Bloomington more than a cat on a tie dye T-shirt with a caption that says, "You can do it. Just focus. You're great." Or how about a squirrel on a motorized scooter? These quirky and loveable prints come on a variety of T-shirts, sweatshirts, hats, buttons, stickers, and more at Badknees. You'll even find gear that supports teachers. Owner Jim Beck spent 13 years teaching public school before focusing on the screen printing biz full-time. Teaching is still near and dear to his heart, so don't be surprised if you see him hosting workshops for students in the future. In the meantime, stop by his shop or shop online for delivery and pickup. You can do it! Just focus!

615 N Fairview St., Unit 5, 812-287-9899
badkneests.com

TIP
Got an idea for a design? Badknees also does custom printing for buttons, magnets, and clothing. Visit the website for a quote.

BUILD A WARDROBE THAT GIVES BACK
AT MY SISTER'S CLOSET

Ladies, imagine a bargain boutique that carries on-trend professional, casual, and formal attire for any occasion . . . a place where the inventory changes daily and the prices on gently-used designer clothing, bags, shoes, and accessories are so low you'll wonder if you're looking at the right tag. On top of all those glowing attributes, My Sister's Closet is also a nonprofit organization that supports women in poverty. By shopping or donating to the store, you're helping their mission to provide free work attire and job skills training to at-risk women seeking employment in the community. Over the years, they have helped thousands of women build wardrobes for success in addition to arming clients with the skills needed to succeed in the workplace. We'll shop to that.

414 S College Ave., 812-333-7710
sisterscloset.org

FIND A TREAT
FOR ANY PERSONALITY
AT POPKORN TWIST

Shopping for someone sweet? How about someone fiery? Find their perfect flavor match at PopKorn, a gourmet popcorn and gift shop that puts a tasty twist on a classic movietime treat. Try Cinnamon Bun or Jalapeno Popper. For coffee lovers, there's Get Buzzed; for Hoosier fans, there's Cream & Crimson; and for those who love to indulge, hook them up with Pecan Karamel Turtle. There are even vegan flavors to share. You'll also find clever popcorn-themed gifts in the brick-and-mortar store as well as their online shop. Founder Dr. Virginia Githiri (known around town as Dr. G) holds multiple degrees in business and public health, but thankfully for her customers, she's also obsessed with making deliciously flavored popcorn. Pop into her downtown shop or visit the kiosk inside College Mall.

122 S College Ave., 812-318-3945
popkorntwist.com

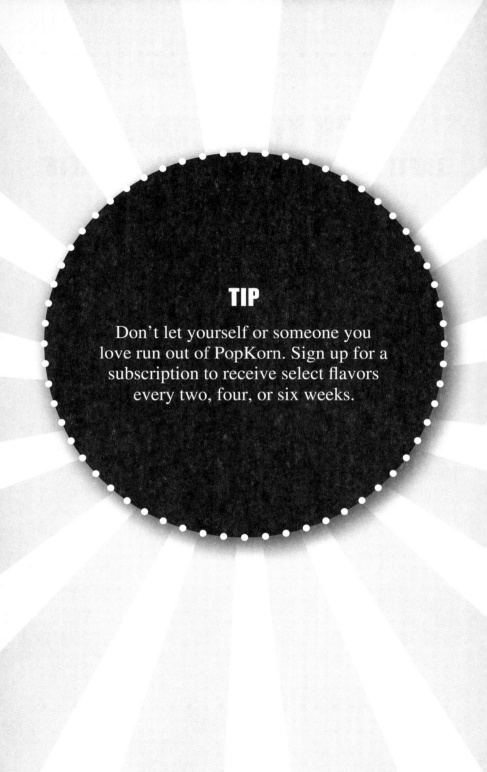

TIP

Don't let yourself or someone you love run out of PopKorn. Sign up for a subscription to receive select flavors every two, four, or six weeks.

DECK YOUR WALLS,
LAPTOPS, WATER BOTTLES, AND JACKETS WITH BLUE ASTER ART

Show the world your love for all things cute, quirky, and natural with fun stickers, pins, and prints. Blue Aster Studio is a Bloomington husband-wife team creating original art reflecting the best of Bloomington's nature scene. Shop for handmade stickers that say "Turtle Crossing Guard" and "Bat's So Awesome" or buttons that say "Totally Opossum" and "Nerdy for Nature" accompanied by loveable designs. You'll also find a selection of tote bags, unique greeting cards, striking screen prints that are numbered and signed, as well as reproduction art prints. In line with their love of nature, the couple practices sustainability when possible by using recycled and compostable materials (and living in a solar-powered home). Look for Blue Aster at local handmade pop-up markets or shop their online store.

blueasterstudio.com

SPRUCE UP THE PLACE
AND LIGHT A GIANT SCENTED CANDLE
AT SIMPLY PRIMITIVE

A stop at Simply Primitive on the southwest side of Bloomington will make you want to redecorate the entire house, kitchen and all. Inside, you'll find multiple rooms of farmhouse decor, from seasonal throw pillows to dining room furniture. One room is dedicated entirely to foodies, with a selection of sauces, jellies, oils, vinegars, baked goods, utensils, serving dishes, and more. Most shoppers can't leave without buying one or more of the many sweetly scented Hilltop candles, which are poured on site and range in sizes (up to two gallons!). During the holidays, the shop is decked out with antique-like decorations that promise to make spirits bright. Whether you're looking for gourmet goodies or you just want to spruce up the house, you'll find something you simply love.

4445 W State Rd. 45, 812-825-9660
facebook.com/simprim

GET YOUR HOLIDAY SHOPPING DONE
AT THE BLOOMINGTON HANDMADE MARKET

Check off everyone on your holiday shopping list while supporting local and regional crafters and artists. It sounds too good to be true, but you can see it for yourself in November at the Bloomington Handmade Market. This two-day juried craft show highlights extraordinary handmade products from Bloomington and around the Midwest. Shoppers can peruse booth after booth of unique arts and crafts, including one-of-a-kind jewelry, clothing, handbags, candles, lotions, home decor (like chandeliers, pottery, and coasters), and so much more. Organizers review countless artist applications to ensure that a variety of media is represented. Although your mission might be to shop for others, good luck not finding something you have to have for yourself.

bloomingtonhandmademarket.com

TIP

Bloomington Handmade Market also does a summer market downtown. Follow them on social media @bloomingtonhandmademarket for event details and updates.

Griffy Lake

SUGGESTED
ITINERARIES

FAMILY ACTIVITIES

NEARBY DAY TRIPS

• •

EXPLORING CAMPUS

GET OUT IN NATURE

• •

ALONG THE B-LINE TRAIL

ART LOVERS

GRAB A DRINK

FOR THE FOODIES

INDOOR ADVENTURES

DATE NIGHT

ACTIVITIES
BY SEASON

SPRING

Play Pickleball in the Park, 75

Buy a Share, Donate a Share at the Farmers Market, 114

Break Away from an Ordinary Sporting Event at the Little 500, 66

Give a Hoot and Find All 12 Limestone Owls on Campus, 100

Tee Off with a Game of Disc Golf, 74

Strike a Pose in Front of the Sample Gates, 58

SUMMER

Eat Fried Catfish at the Porthole Inn, 29

Meander with Local Art Lovers at the 4th Street Festival, 108

Pour Your Own Bear of Honey at Hunter's Bee Farm, 15

Picnic in Style at a Local Winery, 24

Meet Up at Food Truck Friday, 34

Watch the Big Screen under the Stars at the Starlite Drive-In, 35

Ask for Candy Eyes at the Chocolate Moose, 6

Lunch Break Near the Waterfall at Lower Cascades Park, 57

Eat Crêpes from the Window at Le Petit Café, 14

Eat Your Way through an Edible Community Orchard, 61

Make a Splash at the IU Outdoor Pool, 90

FALL

WINTER

• •

The Chocolate Moose

INDEX